HOW TO COMMUNICATE AT WORK

In this Series

Other titles in preparation

could be vital. Always state the company name, your own name and any department name or extension number.

Never keep someone hanging on the line without telling them what you are doing and who you are trying to contact. Many switchboards now operate a **queuing system** where you can listen to music while you wait. This can be irritating, but does at least pass the time.

If the call is not actually for you, try to connect the caller as quickly as you can to the person they wish to speak to. If that person is not available, either ask the caller to ring again, or take their number and pass it on to the person concerned.

Answering the telephone step-by-step

1. Telephone rings.

2. Pick up telephone promptly (within four rings).

3. Say 'Good morning' or 'Good afternoon — Seaview Holiday Caravan Park. Debbie speaking. How can we help you?'

4. Listen carefully to the caller.

5. If the call is for you, deal with it promptly.

6. If the call is for someone else, transfer it.

7. If that person is out, ask if you can take a message, or whether the caller would like to ring again, or whether they would like to be called back when the person wanted returns.

8. Make notes on anything discussed, passing on any messages.

9. Thank the caller for telephoning.

Examples

Patsy and Molly were originally employed as telephonists at Seaview. With the introduction of the latest electronic equipment, however, they are to become general office clerks, the telephone calls being divided between all the staff.

Robert has asked them to help other members of staff, training them to speak correctly on the telephone. They listen in on a couple of calls to see where improvements are needed.

Example 1

Firstly, they listen to Ron Green answering the telephone:

'Hello, who's that? What? I can't hear you very well. It must be a bad line. Who am I? I'm Ron Green, the site foreman. Who did you want? Okay, I'll try and put you through. Don't blame me if we get cut off, though.'

Molly takes down this conversation and then suggests Ron should have spoken as follows:

'Good morning/afternoon. Seaview Holiday Caravan Park. I'm Ron Green, site foreman. How can we help you?

'Sorry, do you think you could speak up? I can't hear you very clearly. Yes, that's better. You wanted to speak to Jim Bruce? Right, I will get you transferred.'

Example 2

Secondly, they listen to Terry Lloyd trying to contact a caravan supplier:

'Hi, it's Terry Lloyd here. I wanted to speak to Dick. Is he in? Not another boozy lunch surely!'

Patsy suggests the following:

'Hello, it's Terry Lloyd from Seaview here. Is Dick in at the moment? No, well have you any idea when he will be back? Right, thanks for your help. I'll call back later.'

Assignment

Working as Molly Wright, draw up some guidelines to give to all staff at Seaview. Use the headings:

> 1   Making a Telephone Call
> 2   Answering the Telephone
> 3   Speaking to the General Public

TAKING A MESSAGE

There will probably be many times in your working life when you will be asked to take a message for someone else. This message may be from a telephone caller or from a caller to the office.

Essential information to note

Messages should contain the following information:

● who the message is for

- whether it was a telephone or personal call

- caller's name

- caller's address or company

- their telephone number

- the message

- whether any action was taken

- name of person who took the message

- the date and time.

Many companies will have their own message pads, which could look something like the one in figure 6.

Details should be accurately recorded. If you feel it is necessary, place a copy of the message in the relevant file as well as giving a copy to the person concerned. Always keep a copy for yourself as proof.

GIVING A TALK

Many individuals find just the thought of standing up and addressing a group of people a terrifying prospect. Although giving a talk for the very first time can be a nerve-racking experience, good preparation should help to minimise any problems on the day.

What sort of talk might you be asked to deliver?

- a talk to prospective customers

- a talk to other employees — training, details of new products

- a talk on behalf of your company at a social event — club, society, special dinner.

First of all, find out where you are to give the talk and how many people will be attending. You should then try to find out something about the type of people who will be listening to you. Are they likely to know more than you do about the subject you are taking on? If

MESSAGE FORM

Message for . . . .

Telephone/Personal Call*

Urgent/Non Urgent*

* delete as applicable

Caller's Name . . . .

Company . . . .

Address . . . .

. . . .

Telephone Number . . . .

Message . . . .

. . . .

. . . .

. . . .

Action to be taken . . . .

Date . . . . Time . . . .

Message taken by . . . .

Fig. 6. Example of a message form.

so, some quick and extensive research is needed. Nothing is more embarrassing than being asked a question to which you do not know the answer.

The length of time you are required to speak is an important factor in the planning stage. It is actually much easier to talk for an unlimited time than to have to fit in say a half hour slot sandwiched between two other speakers or events.

Preparation

Once these decisions are settled you can get down to the actual preparation of your talk. Remember to:

● Prepare your subject thoroughly.

● Make notes to read from — headings rather than the full text.

● Prepare any necessary handouts.

● Arrange for the use of audio visual equipment where necessary, such as flip charts, overhead projectors, video recorders.

● Practise your speech, preferably asking someone to listen to you. Give particular attention to the volume and clarity of your voice.

On the day

How many times have you listened to a talk, nearly fallen asleep and had little or no recollection afterwards of what it was all about? Probably quite often. The aim is for your talk to be amazingly different! Apart from knowing your subject, it needs to be interesting, witty and down-to-earth, in order to hold your listeners' attention.

1. Choose a good start to your talk. The first few minutes will set the scene. Either your audience will warm to you or they will begin to doze off to sleep.

2. Talk with enthusiasm and confidence, throwing in a joke here and there for light relief.

3. Make eye contact with your audience. Let them feel you are really talking to them rather than to yourself.

4. Speak slowly and clearly, and in simple, easy to understand language. Try not to show any nervousness you might be feeling.

5. At the end, give the audience a summing up of the main purpose of the talk and invite them to ask you questions. Make sure you answer these questions as accurately as you possibly can.

6. Finally, try to end on a complimentary, funny or high note and remember to thank your audience for listening to you.

CHECKLIST

● Always speak clearly, simply and accurately.

● Do not use too many long or complicated words.

● Become a skilled listener.

● Ask questions to gain information.

● Be polite and helpful on the telephone.

● Make sure messages taken are accurate.

● Thoroughly prepare the subject for a talk.

● Make sure you know who you will be talking to.

● Make any talk as interesting as possible.

● Remember to thank the audience for listening.

ASSIGNMENTS

For both these assignments imagine you are Susan Jones, office manager.

1. Design a message form to be used specifically in the reception area. It is to record messages left by personal callers for the various members of staff.

2. Prepare notes setting out a formula for the office staff to use when greeting holidaymakers.

POINTS FOR DISCUSSION

1. Write out some tips for a junior on answering the telephone and making telephone calls.

2. List six points to remember when listening to others. State why each is important.

3. Working with a partner, decide on a topic for a talk, about five minutes long. both of you make your own notes and then take it in turns to deliver your talk. At the end you can offer constructive criticism or comments to each other.

3
How to Liaise, Negotiate and Persuade

To get things done at work means working effectively with other people. Those people may include your boss, colleagues, subordinates, customers, suppliers, visitors and others. In your dealings with all these people, it will pay you to learn how to liaise, negotiate and persuade really effectively.

In this chapter we will discuss:

- liaising with colleagues
- negotiating and persuading
- making decisions
- offering advice
- accepting criticism
- learning to delegate

LIAISING WITH COLLEAGUES

One of the dictionary definitions of the word 'liaison' is 'communication and co-operation'. Co-operation, like communication, is a key word in working life. Without co-operation or a good liaison between colleagues, an organisation will not thrive.

A working environment is normally made up of men and women of all ages, from different backgrounds, and with greatly varying personalities. It is very important that a good working relationship is established and maintained. Everyone is human, however, and from time to time tempers will become frayed and a clash of personalities will occur, but the less such negative interaction takes place the better, for everyone.

If you can successfully liaise with your colleagues and build up a good relationship with everyone you work with, you will stand a very real chance of making your working life worthwhile, rewarding and enjoyable!

NEGOTIATING AND PERSUADING

If everyone were able to learn the art of negotiating or bargaining with others, seeing the other person's point of view as well as their own, then business decisions would be made rapidly and well.

You have probably heard the term 'negotiated settlement' often used between trade unions and management. This means a settlement reached by talks, discussions, exchange of thoughts and ideas and often some degree of compromise on both sides.

Similarly, gentle persuasion can often help others to see your point of view, but the emphasis here is on *gentle* persuasion. If you tell a customer that he *must* buy your product, his immediate reaction will be 'No thanks.'

Case study: dealing with customers

Example 1
Jim Bruce, the sales manager of Seaview Holiday Caravan Park, is trying to sell a new caravan to a Mr and Mrs Scott. They are walking round the available caravans, and Jim starts the conversation as follows:

'This model, the Sapphire, could well be in your price range. It's brand new this year. The main bedroom with en-suite bathroom is a particular feature, and look at the kitchen. I think you will agree it is beautifully equipped.' Jim shows them round his favourite, which coincidentally is the caravan he stands to make most commission on.

'I'd like to look round that one over there again,' says Mr Scott. 'I did like the lounge layout, and it's cheaper too, isn't it?'

'Yes it is. Let's take another look. The main difference between the two is in the standard of the fittings. But only you can decide on your priorities and the amount of money you want to spend.' Jim shows them round the other van.

'What would you go for out of the two, Mr Bruce?' asks Mrs Scott.

'Well, I have to say I would go for the Sapphire. It is a new model and will not date so quickly, and I think the layout and standard of equipment is far higher, but that is only my opinion. . .'

Example 2
Mr and Mrs Scott have been gently persuaded that the Sapphire would be their best choice and they decide to buy one, but what would have happened if the conversation had gone differently? If

Jim had not been such an experienced salesman, he might have spoken to them as follows:

'Now this model, the Sapphire, is the one for you. It's brand new this year. The main bedroom with en-suite bathroom is a particular feature and look at the kitchen. I think you will agree it is beautifully equipped.'

'I'd like to look round that one over there again,' says Mr Scott. 'I did like the lounge layout, and it's cheaper too, isn't it?'

'Yes it is, but there is no comparison really. We'll take another look, but the Sapphire is the one for you.'

They go across to the other van, but Jim just stands outside while Mr and Mrs Scott go in.

Jim shouts to them through the door. 'I expect you can see the difference now. This one is very basic and poorly equipped. Are you going to settle on the Sapphire today?'

'No, actually we like this one, and if we decide to buy a caravan here at all, this will probably be the one, but we'll think about it for now,' replies Mr Scott.

Mr and Mrs Scott are annoyed at the high pressure salesmanship. Far from selling the caravan Jim's technique puts them off altogether.

Assignment

If you were Jim Bruce, how would you persuade a couple thinking of up-grading their caravan for a new one at Seaview that it would be a good idea for them to do so? Working with a partner, act out a possible conversation.

MAKING DECISIONS

Many people find it incredibly difficult to make decisions. Do you know some 'ditherers' in your home and in working life, the sort who can never decide on *anything*? It is an unfortunate fact of life, especially for such people, that life is full of decisions.

Try to become a decisive person yourself. A decisive person gets things done. An indecisive person just thinks about getting things done! When making a decision, weigh up the pros and cons carefully, ask for advice from others if necessary, and then go ahead.

The decisions you make in your working life may not always turn out to be the right ones, but as long as you can learn from any wrong decisions, all will not have been lost.

How to reach a good decision

To help you to make the right decision first time, take a look at the suggestions below:

● Assemble the facts relating to the decision to be made.

● Identify the choices available.

● Assess whether anyone else needs to be involved in making the decision.

● Consider the 'risk factor'. What will happen if the wrong decision is taken?

● Select the option with the lowest risk factor, as long as it still satisfies the aim.

● Once the decision is made, act on it as soon as you can.

● Above all, try never to make 'on the spot' or rash decisions that you might regret later on.

Example of a rash decision

Lynn Knight, one of the cleaners, is busy cleaning out a caravan one morning, when she is approached by a holidaymaker from another hire van. He asks her whether their van could be cleaned out an hour later than the stated departure time as his wife is disabled and they will need a little more time to get themselves ready. Lynn, without asking anyone else, tells him that the stated departure time must be respected and that no exceptions can be made.

The man then goes straight to reception and complains. Rose Smith, the cleaning supervisor, deals with the problem by saying that the family can have up to two hours' extra time, which will still enable them to prepare the caravan for the next people. Rose then interviews Lynn, severely reprimanding her for taking such a decision, with neither thought for the couple nor checking with herself as cleaning supervisor.

Comment

Eventually matters are put right, but had Lynn taken advice in the first place rather than making a rash decision on her own, the problem would have been solved immediately.

Assignment

As general manager, you need to make decisions on staffing levels from time to time. Often extra staff need to be taken on during the summer months. What factors would you consider when making such decisions? What advice if any would you seek from your staff?

OFFERING ADVICE

Always try to listen to other people and their problems, but it's better not to offer advice unless asked to do so. This really applies to both your private and working life. Advice offered in good faith can have a habit of being twisted or changed to suit a person's aims.

If you are asked to give your advice on a matter, prepare your answer thoroughly. Remember, the person or persons involved are putting some faith in your judgement, so you must try not to let them down. Advice should be as unbiased as you can make it. If you feel your advice could be biased then you should say so.

You may occasionally be asked to give your advice on a confidential matter. If this is the case, make sure that you *keep* the matter confidential and that you are not responsible for betraying a confidence.

ACCEPTING CRITICISM

There is a big difference between **constructive criticism** and criticism without any purpose. Constructive criticism can be very useful, positive and helpful. Criticism for no reason is destructive.

If you are criticised by a work colleague, first of all stop and think whether the criticism is justified. If it is, do something about it. Never be afraid to admit to yourself that you have made a mistake. We all make mistakes, many times in every single day, and if colleagues spot them and criticise, perhaps it is for the best. It will make you stop and think.

If you honestly feel the criticism is unjustified, challenge the person involved and ask them why they think you are in the wrong. It is an unfortunate fact of life that some people, particularly in high positions, seem to need to justify themselves by continual criticism of those under them. This situation should not be allowed to continue unchecked. If you ever feel you are being victimised in any way at work, you should complain to the appropriate person.

LEARNING TO DELEGATE

All successful managers and bosses have learned to delegate. In big organisations they could not possibly take all the decisions themselves. The dictionary definition of delegate is 'to entrust authority to a deputy', but whatever your position within an organisation, and whether or not you have a deputy, some degree of delegation will probably be helpful.

Why people find it hard to delegate

Delegation can be a problem area. Reasons why managers and others fail to delegate are as follows:

- They think they will do a better job themselves.

- They think they can do a job quicker.

- They do not want to spend the necessary time training someone else.

- They are afraid that someone else might actually do the job better than they can.

- They like to be seen to be overworked.

- They may not be able to delegate due to lack of staff.

Only the last reason is a valid one.

The advantages of delegation

Delegation, if properly carried out, can:

- Improve overall efficiency in the workplace.

- Give all workers a greater sense of purpose.

- Alleviate boredom by giving extra tasks to under-occupied workers.

- Take the pressure off over-occupied workers.

- Create improved teamwork.

- Establish a friendly working environment.

Delegation step-by-step

1. Decide on tasks to be delegated. (Only delegate tasks that can be permanently shifted.)

2. Decide on who you will delegate to.

3. Check on that person's existing workload.

4. Ask that person if they are happy to accept the extra workload.

5. If they are, train them to carry out the tasks.

6. Monitor progress.

7. Delegate further if necessary.

Remember, delegation, particularly amongst managers and specialist staff, means more time for them to concentrate on what they do best and less chance of them suffering from a nervous breakdown or a premature heart attack.

Example: Linda needs to delegate

Linda Grant, personal assistant to Robert Power, has been working much harder of late. Although it is the end of the season, she has taken on extra jobs, delegated by Robert, including organising all the staff holidays, staff working rotas, and most importantly the annual Christmas Dance to which all caravan owners are invited. How can she decrease her workload?

● To start with, Linda can delegate the organising of staff holidays to Susan Jones, the office manager. Susan has far more dealings with the actual staff anyway and is in a good position to speak to them all individually.

● Arranging staff rotas can be delegated to the various heads of department: Susan Jones, Jim Bruce, Ron Green, James Taylor and Rose Smith. Again, not only will this ease the workload for Linda, but it will also result in more efficiency, the relevant heads know their own staff and can plan suitable rotas more easily than Linda can.

These two changes will leave Linda more time to carry out her own important tasks without having to rush through everything and work unreasonably long hours.

ASSIGNMENTS

For both these assignments imagine you are James Taylor, the bar/entertainments manager.

1. Rita Payne, the children's entertainer, has been offered another job. You are desperate not to lose her. Robert says Seaview can give her a small salary increase. Write down what you would say to try to persuade her to stay.

2. John Stein, one of the bar staff, has asked your advice on the deterioration of his marriage. Would you advise him and if so, what would you say?

CHECKLIST

- Learn to consult and co-operate with colleagues.

- Negotiate rather than demand.

- Use the art of gentle persuasion whenever possible.

- Make positive decisions — do not dither.

- Only offer advice if asked to do so.

- Use constructive criticism directed at you to your advantage.

- Learn to delegate whenever you can.

POINTS FOR DISCUSSION

1. Give at least six reasons why you would want to build a good relationship with your colleagues.

2. Are you able to accept criticism from others? Think about some recent instances and summarise how you dealt with them.

3. What benefits can you gain by effective delegation?

4
How to Stand Up for Yourself

Part of being successful at work involves knowing when and how to stand up for yourself. Many people find this quite difficult and daunting, but it is a skill which can be learned. This chapter will discuss some techniques you can use, to help you become more confident in your dealings with the boss, workmates, customers, suppliers and other people you encounter at work.

In particular it will discuss:

- meeting new workmates

- overcoming shyness and insecurity

- coping with a difficult boss

- dealing with sexual harassment

- pacifying an angry customer

- coping with bullying at work

MEETING NEW WORKMATES

When you start a new job, and to a lesser extent when someone else joins your organisation, you will have to meet new workmates.

Some people seem able to fit in anywhere, with anyone, and at any time. The rest of us have to work at it. If you are one of these a few suggestions might help to get you over the first hurdles of starting a new job.

Learning to fit in
- If someone else is doing the introductions, just smile and say hello in a friendly fashion, shaking hands with anyone who offers to do so.

- If you are introducing yourself, say 'Hello, I'm glad to meet you. My name is. . .'

- Wait until you are shown where to sit. Do not make the mistake of sitting in another person's seat. This will not get you off to a good start.

- Be patient if your fellow workmates are not immediately able to show you what you should be doing. They may be busy, with important tasks to do before they can spend some time with you.

- Do not try to 'push in' on other people's conversations. Remember, they may take some time to get used to you.

- Do not give the impression that you are going to 'organise' everyone (unless that is what you have specifically been employed to do).

- Take your time to get to know your new workmates. Do not rush into friendships that you might regret later on.

The age factor

The 'age factor' deserves a special mention here. This particularly applies to women returning to work after bringing up a family, but it could happen in other circumstances too. Never think that because you are much older than other members of staff doing the same job, you are somehow more 'important' than them and can give them orders. If you are returning to work you may well be taking a lower position than you held before, but you will have to work your way back up the ladder. Younger members of staff will immediately resent it if you try to order them about.

Example

Seaview is employing two temps to help in the reception area during August, their busiest month of the year. Both women are in their early forties and have held senior positions in the past. One is called Sheila and the other Mary. It is their first morning and Susan Jones, the office manager, is showing them around the office and introducing them to the other members of staff. The conversation goes as follows:

'Right, Sheila and Mary, I'd like to introduce you to Sally, Patsy and Molly. Sally uses the word processor most of the time, inputting bookings and sending out routine correspondence. Molly and Patsy carry out all the general office duties, and you will be helping them, particularly on the reception side.' Susan ushers Sheila and Mary to some seats as everyone exchanges polite greetings.

'Now, for today, I would like you both to just watch and listen. You will learn a good deal from the others. I will then instruct you tomorrow on what I want you to do on the reception side and you can begin working there on Wednesday. Does that sound reasonable to you both?'

'Yes, thanks Mrs Jones,' says Sheila. 'I was a bit worried about being thrown in at the deep end. A day to observe will suit me just fine. The girls seem to have got a good routine and I wouldn't want to do anything wrong.' Sheila looks very relieved and eager to please.

'Well I suppose it's all right with me too,' says Mary grudgingly. 'I really don't think I shall need much instruction, though. I was running a very large reception office when you must have been still at school.'

'I'm sure you have vast past experience, Mary, but things have changed over the last ten to fifteen years. We do things very differently now you know.' Susan feels annoyed at Mary's obvious reluctance to be shown what to do by someone younger.

Susan gestures to the two ladies that she has finished with them for now and they both get up to observe what is going on in the office. Susan leaves to go and see James Taylor over in the bar.

Molly and Patsy beckon Sheila over to them. They start to explain to her what they are doing and Sheila watches with obvious interest, very keen to let everyone know that she has a lot to learn.

No-one takes any notice of Mary, so she starts to re-arrange the reception area.

Susan returns half an hour later. By this time Mary has rearranged the books, changed the seating and brochures around and is just about to start on the register of new arrivals. She greets Susan with a patronising smile:

'Hello there Susan. I thought I would just make a few changes while you were out. The say a new broom sweeps clean, and I thought my experience might help a little here and there. I hope you don't mind.'

'It is Mrs Jones to you, Mary, not Susan, and yes I *do* mind. We had everything just as we wanted it. We did not need you to rearrange it all for us.' Susan is fuming, absolutely furious that this woman should come in and expect to run the office and dare to tell her, the office manager, that she could benefit from her experience.

Needless to say, Mary only lasts the day. Susan telephones the agency and asks for a replacement. Sheila, on the other hand, proves to be a valuable member of the team. She is eager and capable of learning quickly and soon becomes very popular amongst all the staff.

Mary would do well to learn that her past experience counts for very little when she re-enters today's business world. She has got to prove herself all over again, by learning from those now in the top positions. She must learn to fit in. Eventually she may end up in an even higher position than before, but not without a lot of hard work and the ability to make herself popular with those around her.

OVERCOMING SHYNESS AND INSECURITY

Are you a shy and insecure person? Very many people are. It is very easy to say in a book such as this that if you do x y and z your shyness and insecurity will disappear, as if by magic. Unfortunately, in reality, nothing is that easy. It is possible, however, to examine the reasons why we feel shy and insecure, and to look at ways of slowly overcoming such feelings.

Shyness and insecurity usually stem from childhood experiences. Perhaps we had a parent or a sister/brother who constantly undermined our actions and thoughts. Perhaps we were an only child who spent most of our time at home with the parents, rarely mixing with anyone apart from school friends and relatives. Perhaps we have suffered the break up of a relationship which was very important to us.

A positive approach

There are positive ways of working towards confidence and security:

- First, and most important of all, start to believe in yourself and your abilities.

- *Make* yourself talk to as many people as you can, not necessarily just at work — in a bus queue, at the supermarket, friends and neighbours.

- Look interested in what other people have to say. One of the big problems with shy people is that they often come over to others as being aloof or stand-offish. Try not to give this impression.

- Look at other people, particularly those you think positively ooze self confidence. Are they as confident as they first appear? Underneath it all they are probably just as insecure as you are.

- Finally, take up a hobby, or work towards a goal of some sort. This will build your confidence and will help you to believe in yourself, which as we have already mentioned is the most important step of all.

COPING WITH A DIFFICULT BOSS

Most bosses have the reputation of being 'difficult' in some way or another. Everyone needs a scapegoat when things go wrong and workers tend to blame the bosses, just as bosses tend to blame the workers.

If your boss has his or her difficult ways, it's best to come to terms with the situation and deal with it as best as you can. After all, your boss could have a lot on his or her mind and at times be working under heavy pressure. Be prepared to make allowances for the times when you are shouted at, either because of a mistake you have made, or because you just happen to be around at the wrong time!

If you are picked on

No-one is perfect, and your boss, like everyone else, will have his or her off days. However, if you ever find yourself in a position where you are being continually 'picked-on', to the point where it is making you miserable, then action needs to be taken. First of all, of course, consider whether you could be in the wrong. Perhaps you are acting in a manner which displeases your boss? Or perhaps your work just isn't up to standard? In this case the solution rests with you.

If, on the other hand, you are doing your job to the best of your ability and it is still not considered good enough, then the time has come for you to speak to your boss about the way you are being treated. Sometimes bosses just do not realise the upset and bad feeling they are creating. Sometimes they need to be told in order to do something about it. If this does not work, speak to your boss's superior, if there is one, and if necessary make a formal complaint.

Whilst you should never feel compelled to change your job because of a difficult boss, if all else fails it could be your best option. Life is too short, and work hours too long, for you to accept unhappiness in your working life.

DEALING WITH SEXUAL HARASSMENT

Sexual harassment can conjure up different pictures in people's minds; most would probably think in terms of an amorous male pinching the bottom of a female employee or perhaps looking up her skirt and making unwelcome remarks as she walks up the stairs. The term can, however, cover much more serious incidents than these and men can be victims as well as women.

What sexual harassment means
The European Commission defines sexual harassment as 'unwanted conduct of a sexual nature, or other conduct based on sex affecting the dignity of women and men at work'.

To look at the term more simply, sexual harassment can include the following:

● Uninvited sexual attention.

● Someone making sexual comments or suggestions.

● Any implication that promotion or pay rise will result from sexual favours, or that dismissal could arise if such favours are not forthcoming.

● Material being passed around workers which could upset or offend them.

● Sexual assault and rape.

No person at work should put up with any form of sexual harassment. In most cases the matter can be sorted out between the parties involved, but if the matter becomes serious you can always seek redress under the **Sex Discrimination Act 1975**, and your case would go before an Industrial Tribunal.

What to do if you suffer harassment
If you feel you are the victim of sexual harassment:

● Keep notes of any harassment. Record when and where it occurs.

● **Tell** the person concerned that you are not prepared to tolerate their behaviour. This action in itself will often solve the problem.

- In case the harassment continues, take the precaution of asking your **work colleagues** whether any of them have been harassed by the same person. If they have, ask them to keep a record too.

- If the person continues harassing you or your colleagues **report** them to your immediate superior or your Union. If the harasser is the overall boss and there is no-one else to tell, ask an official body like the Citizens Advice Bureau for their help.

- Remember, the Industrial Tribunal is there should you need it. Don't just put up with the situation.

Example

Terry Lloyd, a general assistant at Seaview, considers himself to be a real 'lad', larking about with the girls and generally having a good time in life. He takes a fancy to Carol, one of the cleaners, and begins to flirt with her, putting his arm round her, pinching her on the bottom and whistling whenever she goes past. Carol is a happily married lady and finds his advances offensive and annoying. She tells him this, but he just laughs.

Matters come to a head when Terry finds her in the linen room, shuts the door, pins her to the wall, and gives her a big kiss. He goes off laughing and Carol collapses in tears. She is too embarrassed to say anything to Rose Smith, the cleaning supervisor, and hands in her notice instead. Carol tells Rose that she is leaving for personal reasons and Rose accepts this.

On the day she is due to leave, Avril, one of the other cleaners who knows about Terry and his amorous ways, tells Rose the real reason. Rose asks to see Carol to check the story and when she is sure of her facts she approaches Robert Power, the general manager.

Robert sees Terry, who is genuinely upset that his actions should have caused so much trouble. He explains that he just likes a bit of fun. Robert warns him that if he ever makes any advances at all to any member of staff in the future, he will be immediately dismissed. Terry promises to be good in future and to apologise to Carol for his actions.

Carol is advised that there will be no further trouble with Terry and she stays at Seaview.

Of course, had Carol taken the matter to Rose immediately, it could have been solved without the need for her to hand in her notice and go through the trauma of thinking she would have to change her job. If the matter is important enough to genuinely upset someone then it is important enough to report to the relevant person.

Assignment

Working with a partner, one of you acting as Robert Power and the other as Terry Lloyd, work out the conversation that would need to take place between you both to make Terry understand that his behaviour would not be tolerated in the future.

PACIFYING AN ANGRY CUSTOMER

There are bound to be moments in your working life when you will have to pacify an angry customer. Don't let yourself become emotional and flustered. Use this technique to manage the situation.

1. The first step is to find out why the customer is angry. Once you know the reason for the anger, check for yourself to see whether the anger is justified. There is a saying 'the customer is always right', and to some extent that is true, but occasionally it will happen that the customer has made a mistake, not your organisation. Should this be the case, explain to the customer, very politely, what you think has happened, and hopefully all should be well.

2. Unfortunately, however, when a customer is angry, he or she usually has a very good reason for that anger. If it transpires that your organisation has made a mistake in any way, you should immediately explain what has happened and offer your apologies.

3. Next, try to rectify the mistake as quickly as you possibly can. Apologies are all very well, but if the matter is not sorted out, the apology will be of little use, and the customer will become even more irate — with good reason.

4. *Never* lose your temper with a customer, even if it turns out that they were in the wrong. If the customer complains to you, *you* are the communication link between your organisation and that customer and you must always be polite, apologetic and reassuring. That way mistakes can be rectified without loss of business in the future.

Example: parents complain about child supervision

Rita Payne, the children's entertainer, receives a complaint about a child returning to the camp soaked through after an outing. The parents complain to her about inadequate supervision. Rita knows that the child was well supervised and had, in fact, caused more trouble than all the other children put together. The child returned wet because she had insisted on spraying a water pistol all over herself — a water pistol her mother had sent on the trip with her.

Rita could handle this two ways:

Rita's first choice

'I'm disgusted, Ms Payne. How could you let my Celia return home in such a state?' Celia's mother glares at Rita, awaiting her reply.

'I'm very sorry, Mrs Abbott, but your daughter was totally out of control during the entire afternoon. Her behaviour was not helped by the water pistol you sent her with. That was how she became wet. She sprayed it all over herself, as well as several other children. Quite honestly, people like you shouldn't have children at all! I've seen you in the club every evening, getting drunk, with Celia sitting there looking bored stiff. You seem keen enough to get rid of her whenever you can. No wonder the child is attention-seeking.'

'How dare you! I shall report to you the manager immediately. My family will leave tomorrow and we shall never ever come to Seaview again. You've got a nerve. . .' Celia's mother storms off.

Not the way to keep customers happy and spending their money in the club every evening!

Rita's second choice

'I'm disgusted, Ms Payne. How could you let my Celia return home in such a state?' Celia's mother glares at Rita, awaiting her reply.

'I'm really very sorry, Mrs Abbott. Celia had a water pistol with her and I'm afraid she sprayed herself with water. She was adequately supervised, but you will appreciate with fifty children to look after, we cannot watch them all for every second. All I can do is apologise for any inconvenience her wet clothes may have caused you.' Rita looks at Celia's mother wondering how Celia has turned out even vaguely normal, with a mother who gets drunk in the club every night and looks a wreck, but she says nothing.

'Well, I suppose these things do happen, and I know my Celia's no angel. Causes me loads of worry she does. Always in trouble of some sort. I suppose you did your best in the circumstances.'

Celia's mother is placated and goes back to the club that night!

COPING WITH BULLYING AT WORK

Sexual harassment can be a form of bullying, but not all bullying has sexual overtones.

Bullying, both at work and at school, has become more and more evident in recent years. Whether bullying is actually on the increase, or people are beginning to talk about it more freely, is not clear. What is apparent is that there are some very unkind people around who gain pleasure from destroying other people's lives. There have been reports of children killing themselves because they cannot stand the bullying any longer, bullying that is carried out by other children. If those children are not stopped they will grow into adult bullies of tomorrow and so the cycle will continue.

Bullying at work often involves a boss and his or her employee/s. Bad bosses can let the power of being a boss go to their heads and they rule all those under them in a tyrannical fashion.

Many bullies come from violent or unhappy backgrounds. They usually pick on one (sometimes more than one) person who seems to be vulnerable for some reason. Perhaps they are slow at their job, or too pretty, or just in the wrong place at the wrong time.

If you are being bullied at work then follow the same procedure as for sexual harassment. Although you will not be able to seek redress under the Sex Discrimination Act, if the case is serious enough it will go before an **Industrial Tribunal**. As with sexual harassment, however, all other possibilities should be tried first to resolve the problem. Bullies are often capable of reforming, once they are made aware of exactly what they are doing to others.

Never be afraid to expose a bully. It is important for you to take action to try and put things right, for your sake and for the sake of anyone else who might be suffering in the same way. If the bully is made to see the error of his or her ways as a result of your exposure, then everyone could end up happy.

ASSIGNMENTS

For these assignments imagine you are Robert Power, general manager.

1. Prepare a short report to give to all staff on bullying and sexual harassment in the workplace. Make sure it sets out all your feelings on the matter and the action that would be taken if any such problems arise at Seaview.

2. A holidaymaker comes storming into your office demanding a refund because the caravan they are staying in is leaking. What steps would you take to deal with this situation?

CHECKLIST

●   Greet new workmates in a friendly manner.

●   Never act as if you know other people's jobs better than they do.

●   Mix with as many different people as possible.

●   Make allowances for a boss's bad days.

●   Always complain about sexual harassment.

●   Know your rights — you deserve to be treated decently.

●   Remember always to treat a customer politely.

●   Report a bully — he or she needs to be stopped.

POINTS FOR DISCUSSION

1. All employees find their bosses difficult. Do you think this statement is true? If so, why?

2. Work with a partner. One of you is the customer complaining about a dining room suite, delivered three weeks late and in a damaged condition. The second person is the supplier. Record a possible telephone conversation.

3. Do you think bullying at work is on the increase? If so, what do you think can be done to stamp it out?

5
How to Use Body Language

Communication is not just about the written and spoken word, or visual images. Human beings also communicate a great deal about themselves by the body language they project, and see in others. Two individuals, for example, may have almost identical qualifications and experience, but through body language one can come across as confident and enthusiastic, while the other can seem nervous and indecisive.

In this chapter we will discuss how to use and how to interpret body language at work, and in particular:

- understanding body language

- giving the right signals

- interpreting signals from others

- showing respect and enthusiasm

- overcoming an 'attitude' problem

- creating signals from others

WHAT IS BODY LANGUAGE?

Body language, sometimes known as **non-verbal communication**, refers to the way we communicate by using different parts of our body rather than the written or spoken word. It is very often the way in which we show the emotional side of our relationships with others. The messages we convey can be deliberate, such as a nod of the head, a smile, a grimace, a shrug of the shoulders, or involuntary such as a shiver. Body language can often convey more meaning than any words that may be spoken.

Examples of body language

Some examples to illustrate the possible use of body language in your everyday life are as follows:

- How do you face the person you are speaking to — do you look at them or away from them?

- What eye contact is involved? Do you look the other person in the eye, or do you look away as you speak?

- How do you sit — do you sit up straight, looking interested, alert and self-confident, or do you slouch down in your chair with your head down, looking bored and unsure of yourself?

- How close do you stand or sit to the person you are speaking to? The closer you are suggests the closer or more confident the relationship.

- What physical contact do you have with other people? Do you shake hands, cuddle them, kiss them?

- Do you 'fiddle' as you talk? Do you drum your fingers, scratch your head?

- How do you nod and shake your head to show agreement or disagreement?

- What are your expressions, such as a smile or a frown?

GIVING THE RIGHT SIGNALS

It is very important that your body language is interpreted the way you want it to be. Other people can be just as perceptive as you and if you show a bored expression or raise your eyes to the ceiling in annoyance, the chances are it will be noticed. If you want to show your annoyance or boredom then that is fine, but sometimes you may need to hide your real feelings and *pretend* to be interested in what someone else is saying, perhaps for the sake of a business deal or because the person talking is important to you for one reason or another.

As a child you were told to think before opening your mouth to speak. In the same way, try to control your body language and make it work for you in an effective and desirable manner. With practice you can send out the right rather than the wrong signals.

INTERPRETING SIGNALS FROM OTHERS

Next time you have to visit your doctor, use the situation to your advantage. Study the other people sitting in the waiting room. Try to imagine their home life, where they live, why they are visiting the doctor. What problems could they have in their home and business life? You are not being nosy. After all, you are not *asking* them, just interpreting the body language they give out. It's amazing just how much you can learn by interpreting signals from others.

The same is true at work. The more you watch and observe your work colleagues the more you will get to know them. Their actions may well speak far louder than their words.

Reading body language at work
There are certain times at work when it is particularly important to study other people's body language:

- When you are chairing a meeting. What do the gestures, movements, and facial expressions of your colleagues tell you about the success or failure of the meeting?

- When you are giving a talk. Has the audience fallen asleep? Is everyone sitting with bored expressions on their faces? Then change direction and make your talk more interesting and stimulating.

- When you are clinching an important business deal. If you watch your customer or client carefully you will be able to judge for yourself whether or not the deal is likely to succeed.

- When you are involved in a personnel matter. Feelings and emotions will show through the words used by your colleagues.

Example: body language at the talent competition
Rita Payne, the children's entertainer, has organised the usual weekly talent competition for teenagers. Two different girls, Sue and Claudia, have sung the same song in the competition. Rita has never had this happen before, and as both of them sang very well, she decides to interview each girl and let the audience judge who should win.

Interview with Sue

'Well Sue, you sang that very well indeed. Now tell me, where do you come from?' asks Rita.

Sue **smiles** at Rita and the audience before answering. 'I come from Blackpool, although I was actually born in Scotland.'

'And how old are you, Sue?' continues Rita.

'Just sixteen. My birthday was yesterday actually,' Sue replies, **shyly glancing** up at the audience, and winning their immediate round of applause and chorus of *Happy Birthday*.

'And what would you like to be when you leave school, Sue? I presume you are still at school?'

Sue **nods** in reply. 'I would like to go into nursing if I can pass enough exams.' She turns to the audience and **giggles** endearingly. 'I have to practise on my poor Mum and Dad at the moment though.'

The audience laugh and the interview finishes with Sue **taking a bow** to very loud applause.

Interviewing Claudia

'And where do you come from, Claudia?' asks Rita.

Claudia **looks down** at the floor appearing to study her feet as she answers:

'London, actually.'

'Good old London,' replies Rita. 'I come from London too. What part?'

'Edmonton, actually,' replies Claudia, **not even glancing** at the audience in front of her.

'And how old are you, Claudia?' Rita presses on feeling as though she is talking into a vacuum.

'Seventeen actually,' Claudia looks up, **unsmiling**, glances at the audience and then **looks down** again.

'Are you still at school, and what are you hoping to do in the way of a career?' Rita hopes to get this interview wound up quickly. She is not disappointed.

'Yes, I'm at school and I don't really know what I want to do afterwards,' comes the reply from Claudia, who is **slouching** her shoulders and looking distinctly **uncomfortable**. The audience give a polite clap and Claudia **shuffles off** the stage.

You can work out for yourself who wins the prize!

Comment

This is an important lesson to learn. Both girls had presumably entered the competition wanting to win, but when it came to the body language and verbal communication to go with the actual performance, Claudia let herself down badly. By looking at her feet all the time, the audience assumed she was just not interested in them, and her lack of any smile together with her poor answers to the questions, lost her the competition. Sue, on the other hand, captivated the audience by her expressions, apparent happiness and eagerness to please.

SHOWING RESPECT AND ENTHUSIASM

Showing respect and enthusiasm for others and their ideas is revealed as much by the use of body language as by any words we utter.

A child can say, 'Sorry, Dad, I didn't mean to be rude', whilst grinning at his older sister and making rude gestures behind Dad's back. The body language cancels out the spoken words. The child is not sorry at all. On the other hand, if the same child says 'Sorry, Dad, I didn't mean to be rude', facing his Dad and looking down at the ground with a guilty expression on his face, we are led to believe that the child is genuinely sorry for his actions.

Getting back to your working life, you should always show respect for your fellow colleagues. Enthusiasm will not, of course, always be so easy, especially if it is enthusiasm for ideas which you do not inwardly feel enthusiastic about. No-one will realistically expect you to be enthusiastic all the time about everything, however. In fact over enthusiastic people can be very wearing, particularly those who walk around with a permanent grin on their face. No-one can be *that* happy all the time!

Just try to show the right degree of enthusiasm whenever you feel it is justified and proper to do so.

Example: body language and the new recruit

A new employee called Julie joins the organisation. This is an example of how positive body language, and positive words, can together produce a positive result.

The positive example

1. Julie joins your organisation.

2. She is greeted by a member of staff, who introduces himself with a smile and a handshake.

3. The same member of staff introduces Julie to everyone else.

4. Everyone shakes Julie's hand and smiles in a welcoming way.

5. Julie feels nervous, and asks a lot of questions.

6. No one acts as if Julie is a nuisance. Her questions are answered willingly, and with friendly facial expressions.

7. Everyone says 'goodbye' and 'see you tomorrow' when Julie leaves for the evening.

8. Julie goes home after her first day feeling happy and confident about the future.

The negative example

1. Julie joins your organisation.

2. She is greeted by a member of staff with a formal introduction and handshake but no smile.

3. The same member of staff introduces Julie to everyone else.

4. Everyone shakes Julie's hand politely and walks away, without smiling.

5. Julie feels nervous and asks lots of questions.

6. Julie's questions are answered, but with frowns and expressions that suggest she is being a nuisance.

7. Everyone says 'goodbye' and 'see you tomorrow' when Julie leaves for the evening, although she feels from their faces that they would prefer her not to return.

8. Julie goes home after her first day feeling unhappy and dejected about the future.

COPING WITH AN 'ATTITUDE' PROBLEM

You have probably heard the expression, 'Oh, he/she has an attitude problem.' What exactly do we mean? The dictionary defines 'attitude' as 'a way of thinking and behaving'. An attitude problem therefore means that the person in question thinks and behaves in a manner that is unacceptable to others.

Check your attitude

Could *you* have an 'attitude' problem? Are you guilty of any of the following?

- Do you resent being told what to do?

- Do you resent being told how to do something, even if you don't know how to do it by yourself?

- Do you resent authority in any shape or form?

- Do you turn up late for interviews and dress in scruffy clothes?

- Did you dislike school?

If your answers are 'yes' to at least four of these questions, then you probably do have something of an attitude problem, which will soon communicate itself to others.

Such problems can often, though not always, stem from childhood. A child from an unstable background, or one who has had to compete with brainy, personality-plus brothers and sisters, could well grow up with an attitude problem.

Building a positive attitude

Once an attitude problem takes a hold it is very difficult to break. If you have such a problem the following suggestions could help to sort it out.

- First, identify the reason or reasons why you feel the need to 'kick' against society.

- Next, ask yourself what you are gaining from your actions.

- If you feel you do have something to gain, then fine, carry on as you are. If, however, you are honest with yourself and see that your attitude to others is getting you nowhere, then make up your mind it is time for a change.

- Next time someone asks you to do something or gives you an instruction of any sort, try to perform the task as well as you possibly can.

- Try this for a month and then assess the results.

If you do manage to 'kick the habit' you will soon become a more respected and approachable person. That in turn should make your working life more enjoyable and rewarding.

Example: Adam and Cliff reveal different attitudes

Jim Bruce needs some extra help to cover for him when he is on holiday. Robert Power knows two young men who are between jobs and he sends them both along to Jim for him to choose which one to take on. The men are called Adam and Cliff. Jim speaks to each of them in turn about how they would deal with customers interested in buying a caravan.

Adam

'Well, I'd ask them what they are looking for. Most of them are only time-wasters anyway, aren't they?' He looks scornfully at Jim as he answers.

'Everyone has to be treated as a potential customer, Adam, whether they buy in the end or not. Do you understand what I'm saying?' Jim is pretty sure that Adam doesn't and his answer communicates it.

'Sure I understand, but I don't agree with you. If I work here it's up to me to decide how to treat the customers, isn't it?' Adam looks across at Jim disdainfully. He tilts his chair back and starts to look out of the window.

'I don't think we would be on the same wavelength if you came to work here, Adam. I'm sure you would be better suited elsewhere.' Jim can't wait to get rid of this self-opinionated young man.

Cliff

'Well, I'd leave them to browse for a while, rather than pounce on them. Then I would quietly approach and ask if I can be of any help to them,' replies Cliff, sitting upright in his chair and looking enthusiastic at the possible challenge.

'Good,' replies Jim. 'Then what would you do?'

Cliff smiles at Jim, establishing eye contact, as he replies: 'I'd do my very best to sell them one of our caravans.'

Jim smiles back, impressed at Cliff's attitude. Just on that short exchange he knows that Cliff will be the right man to stand in for him.

Assignment

Working as the sales manager, make a list of the language you think would be important when talking to a potential customer.

CREATING SECURITY AND SPACE

In your working life you will usually find that space is related to status. The higher up the working ladder you go, so your space will increase. The top executive will generally have a spacious office or even a suite of offices, whilst the poor little clerk will probably only have the space that he or she actually occupies with a desk and chair.

However small your working space is, the chances are that you will treat it as your own personal territory. In much the same way as we tend to erect a fence all around our property at home, just to show it is ours, so your desk/work station, bin or machinery will become part of your security. Whilst in your own territory you will feel at ease, anyone else spending too much time there will seem like an 'invader'.

Space is also important when it comes to business relationships. How close you stand when talking to a business colleague will suggest how well you know them. If someone moves closer than you think is appropriate, you will probably object and become tense, wondering why they are acting in such a way.

In one way or another we all need to feel secure. It is just as important for us to know we have our own personal space at work as it is at home.

ASSIGNMENTS

For these assignments imagine you are working as James Taylor, the bar/entertainments manager.

1. One of your bar staff has an 'attitude' problem when dealing with female customers, whom he does not treat with respect. How would you deal with this?

2. You have taken on a temporary girl who is very shy. How would you instruct her in the successful use of body language to help her to project herself?

CHECKLIST

- Do you give the right impression from your own body language?

- Have you studied the body language of other people at work?

- Do you show respect and enthusiasm for others and their ideas?

- Do you have an 'attitude' problem?

- If so, are you going to do anything about it?

- Have you identified your personal space at work?

- Do your workmates ever invade your space?

- If so, are you bothered about it?

POINTS FOR DISCUSSION

1. Do you think body language is important? Give reasons for your answer.

2. How could an 'attitude' problem affect your future job prospects? Give some examples.

3. Spend some time studying someone close to you and see how much they rely on body language as a means of communication. Make a list of what you observe.

6
How to Deal with Visitors

Most organisations receive a regular flow of visitors of various kinds, and we need to be able to communicate well with them all. In this chapter we will discuss:

● receiving and assisting visitors

● giving a good impression

● showing you know your job

● offering refreshment and hospitality

● covering for absent colleagues

● being aware of security

RECEIVING VISITORS

Depending on the type of organisation involved, visitors may be seen by appointment only, or they could be coming and going all day long, with and without appointments.

Keeping an appointments diary
If you work for an organisation where you are involved in making appointments and seeing visitors, keep an appointments diary. In it write full details of the names of your visitors, their appointment times and why they are coming to see you.

If you are making the appointments for your boss it is a good idea to keep two diaries, one for him/her and one for yourself. Make sure all appointments are entered in both diaries, check your own copy every day to make sure that you are not placed in the embarrassing situation of greeting someone whose appointment has been forgotten.

How to make appointments

When making appointments various points should be borne in mind:

● Never make appointments for early morning, unless specifically requested. You or your boss will need that first half hour or so to open the post, sort out any problems, drink lots of tea and coffee, and generally get to grips with the day ahead!

● If you are making appointments on behalf of someone else always check to make sure that person is available at the requested time.

● Make sure you allow sufficient time between appointments. Remember to allow for lunch breaks and any commitments for that particular day.

● Do not break an appointment unless absolutely necessary. If you must, give the other person as much notice as you possibly can.

● Always write down the details of an appointment as soon as you have made it. Never rely on memory.

The most important point to remember, however, is to greet all visitors — whether they have an appointment or not — with a friendly smile. Make each one feel that they are welcome visitors to your organisation.

GIVING A GOOD IMPRESSION

The first impression a visitor normally has is when he or she walks through the door into the reception area. It stands to reason, therefore, that the reception area and everyone in it should communicate a welcome to that visitor. That first impression may well be a lasting one.

The reception area

Reception areas vary greatly, but all should be:

● clean and tidy

● purpose designed

- equipped with chairs, tables, pleasant soft furnishings, magazines, and possibly plants and/or a fish tank

- manned by pleasant, well mannered and smart staff

Some reception areas will be huge and permanently run by receptionists. Others will just be glorified 'entrance halls', where someone will keep watch from another room, or perhaps a buzzer will be set off when the visitor walks in. Either way, as long as the visitor walks into somewhere attractive, is greeted promptly on arrival and dealt with in an efficient manner, the scene will be set for a successful meeting.

Example: Greeting a visitor who arrives at the Seaview reception area

'Good morning, sir. Welcome to Seaview. How may I help you?' Patsy smiles at the man as she speaks.

'Yes, good morning. I've come to see Robert Power. Is he in?' The man has an air of authority about him.

'Yes, he is, sir. Can I ask if you have an appointment with him?' Patsy has not been notified of any appointment for Mr Power that morning.

'No I don't, but if you tell him John Bright is here, I'm sure he will see me.' The man stands towering over the top of the reception counter.

'If you would like to take a seat then, Mr Bright, I will go and speak with Mr Power. Can I offer you a coffee whilst you are waiting?' Patsy knows there could be a delay and she thinks a coffee will help to pass the time.

'No thanks. I've just had one. I'll just sit over here and have a read of one of your brochures.' The man seats himself in the corner and Patsy hurries off to find Mr Power, leaving Sally in charge of the reception while she is gone.

Patsy locates Mr Power and comes back to fetch Mr Bright.

'Mr Bright, Mr Power says he will be delighted to see you. Will you follow me please?' Patsy takes Mr Bright to Robert Power and then returns to reception, having dealt with the visitor in a fully satisfactory manner.

Assignment

Design a reception area that you think would be suitable for Seaview Holiday Caravan Park.

SHOWING YOU KNOW YOUR JOB

When a visitor comes to see you, he or she will usually be looking to find out something about either your organisation in general, or a product/service you offer. It is therefore extremely important for you to show that visitor that you know not only your own job, but also the workings of your organisation and those products/services which you offer.

Before your visitor arrives make sure that you have read the appropriate files, checked up on relevant facts, and generally researched all the information you need for your meeting. Nothing is more off-putting, for both of you, than to have a visitor asking questions you cannot answer. Obviously, however, this situation will arise very occasionally, because meetings are not rehearsed beforehand, but this should be very rare if you prepare yourself well in advance.

Example

A representative called Simon Price has called to see Rose Smith, the cleaning supervisor. Simon's company has just begun marketing a special cleaning fluid; he has come to see Rose about Seaview being used as 'guinea pigs' for trying out this new fluid, free of charge. The meeting goes quite well until Simon starts to ask Rose specific facts and figures:

'Now, Rose, how many cleaners do you have and how many caravans do they each clean in one week?' asks Simon.

'Well, there are five cleaners, but I'm not quite sure how many caravans they each clean. A couple of them work less hours than the others. I will have to check up on that for you.' Rose feels uncomfortable, knowing she should have these facts readily available.

'Okay, we can come back to that later. Now, how many bottles of your present Gusto liquid do you use in one week?' Simon continues.

'About twelve, I suppose, although I will have to check that one too, I'm afraid.' Rose starts to make notes.

'And would all your girls be happy about charting the results of our new product?'

'Oh yes, I'm sure they will,' Rose feels she can answer that one fairly safely, much to her relief.

'Good. Now I will need to know how many caravans you have in total and how that total breaks down into different makes and models. You may remember me mentioning this over the phone when we fixed the appointment?' Simon waits for Rose's answer.

'I'm sorry, Simon. I have been so busy these last few days. I will have to give you a ring with all this information. Will tomorrow be all right?' By this time Rose is feeling very guilty at her lack of preparation for this meeting.

'Well, it's a shame because I had hoped to start you off on the first trial while I was here. Never mind, though. Perhaps we can fix another appointment for next week when you have given me all I need in the way of facts and figures.' Simon is not really happy with the situation but feels he has no option but to leave the matter there for now.

This offers a good example of what happens when a meeting has not been properly planned. We know from the conversation that Rose received ample preparation time for at least one of the questions. She should have made sure that the information needed to answer any likely questions was readily to hand. Instead, another meeting has to be arranged, costing extra time and money for both sides.

OFFERING REFRESHMENT AND HOSPITALITY

All visitors should be made to feel welcome, both when they arrive and during their stay. It is polite to offer some light refreshment, particularly if the visit is to be a long one, or if there has been a delay in seeing the person involved. Tea or coffee, with a few biscuits, can help a visitor to settle in and feel as though they belong.

You may be in a position where you are expected to take business clients out to a pub or a restaurant for more substantial refreshments. As a result of the recent recession in business and industry, however, this does not happen as often as it once did.

If you do take a visitor out somewhere, do make sure the establishment is suitable for your needs. Get to know the pubs and restaurants close by. Choose places where you can talk to your visitor without deafening music. Make sure the food is edible and not too 'way out'. The last thing you want is for a visitor to be suffering from food poisoning the day after going to lunch with you!

Whatever form your hospitality takes, never give a visitor the impression that your organisation is 'stingy'. On the other hand it is not a good idea to get the reputation of being someone who is 'good for a free meal', rather than to do business with.

COVERING FOR ABSENT COLLEAGUES

Sooner or later you will have to see a visitor on behalf of an absent colleague. You may know in advance that the colleague is absent, or you may be in the embarrassing situation of covering for a colleague who has gone missing for some reason.

- Whatever the circumstances, offer your apologies to the visitor for your colleague's absence, and then try to help in any way you can. It may be that you just cannot deal with the matter the visitor has come to discuss, in which case offer another appointment or suggest that your colleague contacts the visitor on his or her return.

- If, however, you can discuss the matter involved — and the visitor is quite happy to deal with you instead of your colleague — then go ahead with the meeting and do the best you can.

- Always take notes on what you discuss. When your colleague returns you can give him or her a full account of all that was said. Your message should also contain details of the date and time of your meeting and any decisions taken. Find out how much responsibility you can assume in such a situation, depending on who you are covering for.

- It is important to remember who you are representing — not only your colleague, but also the organisation for whom you work. It is in everyone's interest to work together and to help each other out on such occasions. Otherwise visitors will leave, dissatisfied with the treatment they have received, and they will probably take their business elsewhere in the future.

Example: the two visiting agents

Two caravan manufacturing agents arrive to see Jim Bruce. The following conversation takes place when the men enter Patsy's reception area.

'Hello there. I'm Roger Bean and this John Rook. We're from Central Caravans. Jim Bruce is expecting us. Could you please tell him we're here?' Roger extends his hand to Patsy, who looks a little flustered.

'Good morning gentlemen. If you would like to take a seat for a moment, I will bleep Jim for you.' Patsy is sure that she saw Jim go out in his car, only a few minutes before, but she tries paging him just the same.

There is no answer from Jim's bleeper. The men begin to show signs of restlessness. Patsy offers them a cup of tea and then tries ringing round to locate Jim. She is unsuccessful.

'I'm really sorry to keep you waiting like this.' Patsy feels increasingly uncomfortable. Reception usually keeps a list of Jim's appointments, although he has been known to forget on occasions in the past.

'Well, why isn't Jim here if he is expecting us?' ask Roger, feeling this a reasonable question to ask.

'I just don't know, I'm afraid. It's possible he has been called away on something urgent.' Patsy tries to cover up.

'In that case he should have told you in the office where he was going, so that you could tell us,' replies Roger, becoming increasingly irritated. 'So you have no idea at all when he will be back then?'

'Well, no, er, could I possibly make you both another appointment, or could Jim come and see you? Wait a minute, I will see if Mr Power is available. He might be able to help.' Patsy offers the best she can.

'No, forget it,' says Roger. 'Come on John, we're wasting our time here. You can tell Jim that we couldn't wait any longer. That caravan he wanted on display will have to go to Greenleaves now. I had said he could have first refusal, but as he isn't here, I shall now go and offer it to them.'

The two men leave, completely dissatisfied with their visit.

Comment

It is a fairly easy task to sort out what went wrong here.

1. Firstly, Jim obviously relies far too much on his memory, which does not perform too well under pressure.

2. He does not always notify the girls of his appointments and on this occasion he even forgot about the appointment himself.

3. When the appointment was made, Jim should have entered it in his diary. (He likes to keep his diary himself rather than give it to his secretary.)

4. Then, on the day of the appointment he should have given details of the appointment time to the girls in reception, so that they would have been expecting the two men.

5. Finally, he should have been close to the reception area at the appropriate time to meet the men as soon as they arrived.

As a result of Jim's poor memory, the display caravan he wanted is to go elsewhere.

BEING AWARE OF SECURITY

Most organisations today are fully aware of the need for good security. In some, where top secret or highly confidential documents are housed, even more than the normal amount of vigilance is necessary.

Keeping a record of visitors

It is important to keep some sort of record of visitors' arrivals and departures, so that should a theft or a breach of confidentiality occur, it will show at a glance who was on the premises at the time. It is quite common for visitors to sign a visitors book, usually kept in the reception area, giving details of who they are, where they come from, who they have come to see and their time of arrival and departure. Some organisations will issue their visitors with a badge, usually just saying VISITOR, so that everyone knows they are not a member of the regular workforce.

Confidential papers

It is essential to keep confidential papers and files out of the way of visitors. They should be locked away in a filing cabinet or drawer. A visitor could, for instance, be waiting in an office for you to arrive to see them. It would be quite natural for that visitor to lean over and try to read some confidential material that you have left lying on your desk. Don't let this happen. Apart from anything else this material could contain details of what the two of you had planned to discuss and it could affect the visitor's judgement before discussions even began.

Many organisations tend to be rather lax about security. This is a big mistake as a breach of security often causes all sorts of unnecessary worry for everyone concerned.

ASSIGNMENTS

For these assignments imagine you are Molly Wright in the reception area of Seaview Holiday Caravan Park.

1. A visitor has come to see Mr Power without an appointment. Mr Power says he does not want to see him. How would you deal with this situation?

2. Design a poster to be displayed in the reception area, telling visitors what to do if the reception area is unattended when they arrive.

CHECKLIST

● Greet all visitors promptly and with a welcoming smile.

● Remember that first impressions are very important.

● Enter all appointments in an appointments diary.

● Make sure the appointment is being made for a convenient day and time.

● Gather all the relevant information before meeting a visitor.

● Offer the appropriate refreshment and hospitality.

● If covering for an absent colleague, remember to apologise to the visitor.

● Make notes to give to the absent colleague on his/her return.

● Record the arrival and departure times of visitors.

● Be aware of the need for good security at all times.

POINTS FOR DISCUSSION

1. How can the use of body language make a visitor feel welcome? Give four examples.

2. Why is it important to look after visitors properly? Suggest three benefits to the organisation.

3. Do you think security is taken seriously enough at work? Explain the reasons for your answer.

7
How to Communicate on Paper

The previous chapters of this book have been mainly concerned with communicating with people face to face. But written communication is also very important in almost every organisation. In this chapter we will discuss:

- why is written communication so important?

- choosing the right words

- selecting the right equipment

- producing a business letter

- writing notes and messages

- compiling a report

- using a form

- using invoices, statements and orders

- preparing a curriculum vitae for job-hunting

WHY IS WRITTEN COMMUNICATION SO IMPORTANT?

The main reason why written communication is so important in the business world is because it provides a **permanent record** of the information supplied. A copy can be kept for future reference by both the sender and receiver.

Written communication is also important because:

- It enables complex subjects to be fully explained.

- It enables copies to be sent to several people.

- It enables the contents to be planned and drafted in advance.

CHOOSING THE RIGHT WORDS

It is vital to choose the right words for your written communication in order to achieve the desired results.

To start with, think about who you are communicating with.

- Is the communication formal or informal?

- Should the communication contain technical language or not?

For instance if the person you are writing to has no technical knowledge of your business, then it would be silly to send them a very technical letter. It usually pays to keep the language as simple as possible, no matter who you are communicating with. Using complicated words can cloud the meaning for the reader.

Always plan your written communication. Make an outline of the points you want to make; prepare a first or draft copy and then a final copy. Read your work through carefully at each stage — have you really explained yourself clearly and accurately? Make sure of your facts before you commit them to paper.

If you have trouble with sentence construction, grammar, punctuation and spelling, then Chapter 12 will help you with basic English.

SELECTING THE RIGHT EQUIPMENT

Technology has changed so much in recent years that it is often hard to decide which equipment to use and when.

The four most important pieces of equipment to use for written communication are as follows:

- the typewriter

- the word processor

- electronic mail

- the fax machine.

The typewriter

The typewriter itself has undergone a transformation. We have moved on from the days of manual typewriters and messy ribbons. We now have sophisticated electronic machines with a memory which lets the operator correct mistakes automatically, as well as perform other functions with apparent ease. Many of the very advanced electronic machines are now classed as word processors. A word processor is a machine which can produce, edit and store documents. Text can be viewed on a screen, albeit a small one, and reproduced at the touch of a button.

The computer using word processing programs

Most often text production (word processing) takes place using a computer and a word processing software program. Word processing programs such as **WordPerfect 5.1** have revolutionised office life and the role of the secretary. The typing part of the secretary's day has been much simplified by the use of such programs leaving the secretary free to become more of a personal assistant or administrator. In the future secretaries as such may disappear altogether. Many personnel are now doing their own correspondence and this will become more widespread as the years go by.

How it works
Most simple word processing programs should enable the operator, amongst other things, to:

- spellcheck the work

- correct text

- delete or add text

- store text

- centre text

- justify text

- rearrange text

- add headers and footers

- display material in columns

- change line spacing and pitch size

- merge names and addresses with standard letters

There is no need for any text to be printed out until the operator is satisfied that it is perfect. Then as many copies as needed can be printed, either in draft copy, which is quicker to print but harder to read, or in best copy quality. Never use draft quality printing if the communication is to be sent to someone else.

Aside from word processing programs, many other programs can be used on a computer, including **spreadsheet** packages for tables and accounts, and **database** programs to act as a computerised filing cabinet.

Electronic mail

Many organisations are now using their computers, linked by a telephone line, to send messages to other organisations in this country and abroad. This is known as **electronic mail** (or **E-mail**) and it will eventually replace the older telex system where two keyboards were linked by telephone line to give a typed message to the receiver.

How it works

The new system works as follows: the sender types a message which is transmitted to the receiver's computer. It can be displayed on both the sender's and the receiver's screen and a copy can be printed out if required. The advantage over the old method is that text can be edited and changed, which was not possible before.

Both the old telex system and the new electronic mail are very useful for sending messages at any time of the day or night. This is particularly beneficial when sending messages abroad where time differences can apply. For instance when it is 12 midday in England it is 12 midnight in New Zealand.

The fax machine

The fax or facsimile machine works in a similar way to the electronic mail system. Instead of two computers being linked by a telephone line, two fax machines which are like photocopiers are linked by the telephone line. The fax machine is used for transmitting text; it is especially useful for sending drawings, diagrams, or legal documents.

SEAVIEW HOLIDAY CARAVAN PARK
Plydmouth
West Sussex
BN21 7YH
Tel: 01234-751239

Your Ref: BYC/345

1 March 199-

The Manager
Select Signs Ltd
STEBBING
West Sussex
BN45 8YN

Dear Sir

SIGNS FOR ENTRANCE TO PARK

With reference to the brochure you sent to us recently, we should be very interested to see samples of your signs.

Our particular interest is in your wooden signs, and we would require two large mounted signs to place at the entrance to the park, giving directions to new arrivals. We enclose a rough sketch showing the approximate wording.

Perhaps you would be kind enough to give us a ring so that we can make arrangements for you to visit us to discuss the matter in more detail.

Yours faithfully

Robert Power
GENERAL MANAGER

enc

Fig. 7. A fully blocked letter with open punctuation.

How it works
The system works as follows: the sender places the original copy on the fax machine which changes it into a series of electronic impulses. These impulses are fed into the telephone line. At the other end, a second fax machine converts the impulses back into a replica or facsimile of the original.

PRODUCING A BUSINESS LETTER

A business letter is the most common form of written communication. You might think that this means business letters are well written because everyone has a lot of practice, but in most cases this is not so.

Rather like a telephone call and greeting a visitor, so a business letter gives the receiver either a good or bad impression of the organisation it represents. A business letter should be:

- well presented
- brief and to the point
- accurate
- easy to read and understand.

Planning in paragraphs
As with all other written communication, decide first on the purpose of your letter and what you want to achieve. Then make a short list of the points to be covered and prepare a rough draft. Start a new paragraph for each new topic.

Your letter should contain an opening paragraph which sets the scene for the rest of the letter. The main points to be covered should be sub-divided into further paragraphs. The final paragraph normally contains a summing-up of the contents and any recommendations. Do not make your sentences or paragraphs too long.

Keeping copies
It is usual company policy to keep a copy of any letter produced. This can then be placed in the relevant file for future reference.

Laying out your letters
Most letters are now produced with what is known as the **fully blocked** layout, and using **open punctuation**, which means no punctuation at all except in the main body of the letter. An example is shown in figure 7.

SEAVIEW HOLIDAY CARAVAN PARK
Plydmouth
West Sussex
BN21 7YH
Tel: 01234-751239

20 April 199-

Mr S Shreeve
Careful Plants Ltd
3 Coronation Road
Brighton
Sussex BN12 8YN

Dear Mr Shreeve,

PLANTS

We would like to buy some plants from your company for our reception area. We need about six big one's and six small one's.

Can you tell us how much the plants will cost and when you can deliver them to us.

Thanks.

Yours sincereley

Susan Jones
OFFICE MANAGER

Fig. 8. Letter requesting information — poor example.

Notes

1. One clear line of space should be left between reference, date, name and address, above and below the subject heading, and between paragraphs. Four clear lines of space should be left for a signature.

2. In this example there is only a 'Your Ref'. Many letters contain an 'Our Ref' and 'Your Ref'.

3. The Post Town, in this case Stebbing, should appear in capitals.

4. In the course of the letter an enclosure is mentioned (the rough sketch). At the end of the letter, after the signature block, leave one clear line space and type 'enc'.

Letters, as in the example in figure 7, should explain exactly what action is required. The next two examples (figures 8 and 9) show the difference between a badly worded letter, giving little information to the receiver, and an effectively worded letter which should bring the correct response.

Examples

Molly Wright has been asked to prepare a letter from Susan Jones to a plant company asking for information about plants for the reception area. The first letter (fig. 8) shows her unsuccessful attempt. Susan reads the letter through and decides to rewrite it. The second letter (fig. 9) shows her improved version.

Notes: Fig. 8

1. Molly has not put the Post Town, Brighton, in capitals.

2. She has not put the postcode on a separate line.

3. A comma has been incorrectly inserted after 'Dear Mr Shreeve'. Apostrophes have been incorrectly inserted in 'ones'.

4. The subject heading 'Plants' is too vague.

5. The letter is poorly worded, not giving the company any real information, yet expecting immediate prices and delivery dates.

6. 'Thanks' does not read well at the end of a letter!

7. 'Sincerely' is spelt wrong.

SEAVIEW HOLIDAY CARAVAN PARK
Plydmouth
West Sussex
BN21 7YH
Tel: 01234-751239

20 April 199-

Mr S Shreeve
Careful Plants Ltd
3 Coronation Road
BRIGHTON
Sussex
BN12 8YN

Dear Mr Shreeve

PLANTS FOR OUR RECEPTION AREA

We would like your company to supply us with several plants for our reception area.

At present we have mainly ferns and geraniums, with one or two large Creeping Figs. These have all become overgrown and need replacing. In all we shall require six large and six small plants, and it would probably be a good idea to keep to similar types to those we have at the moment, if this is possible.

The best idea would be for you to call in and see us, so that you can see for yourself what we require. We shall then require approximate costings and delivery times before making our final decision.

Please telephone before calling to make sure that I am available to see you.

Yours sincerely

Susan Jones (Mrs)
OFFICE MANAGER

Fig. 9. Letter requesting information — better example.

8. There is no mention of whether Susan Jones is Miss, Mrs or Ms, very irritating when writing back.

Notes: Fig. 9
1. The purpose of the letter is clear.

2. The company involved will know exactly what action to take.

Preparing envelopes

Most letters will need an envelope or label ready for mailing. Often **window envelopes** are used, in which case the name and address on the letter must be positioned in a set place; if the letter is folded correctly the address will show through the window.

Unless preparing a window envelope, start the address about half way down and one third across. Always set out the name and address exactly as on the letter. If a heading such as 'Confidential' appears in the letter, remember to show it on the envelope too. An example is shown in figure 10.

CONFIDENTIAL

Miss Sally Smith
Weigh-it-all Ltd
65 The Street
ROSEWAY
West Sussex
BN23 6HN

Fig. 10. Addressing an envelope.

WRITING NOTES AND MESSAGES

Informal notes

If you need to get a message to a business colleague within your organisation, and he or she is not available to speak to, then a hand-written or typed note can be left for them to see on their return.

This note, even if it is handwritten, should be clear and easy to read. It should give the date and time, your name, and the name of the person to whom you are writing. See figure 11.

12 April 199-

1530 hrs

Dear Susan

A Mrs White 'phoned this morning and I asked her to call this afternoon hoping you would be back. She has just called again and says she must speak to you urgently. She wouldn't leave a message. If you get back later today please give her a ring on 0293-621083.

Thanks

Sally.

Fig. 11. A clearly written handwritten letter.

86

Writing newsletters, advertisements and notices

Newsletters
Many large organisations produce a regular newsletter giving details of company activities, staff changes, new products, incentive drives etc. A newsletter will keep all staff in touch with what is going on.

If you are asked to produce a newsletter, remember the following principles:

● Present the newsletter in an attractive way (*eg* layout, headings, illustrations).

● Make it fun to read rather than just a list of tedious facts.

● Keep it as short as possible: don't waffle.

● Make sure all news is included.

Advertisements
You may be asked to place advertisements in newspapers, giving details of job vacancies, new products, or details of your organisation. When designing an advertisement make sure you:

● Make it eye-catching, immediately explaining what it is about.

● Keep it short — extra words can cost a great deal of extra money.

● Check with the papers for any special offers on advertising rates.

● State whether replies should be in writing or by telephone. Include a personal name, the company name, address and telephone number as appropriate.

Notices
You may be asked to prepare a notice for the organisation's notice board. Like advertisements they need to be well displayed and eye catching. They must contain all relevant information, appropriately worded, and any action to be taken should be clearly explained.

```
            Seaview Holiday Caravan Park
            Plydmouth   West Sussex BN21 7YH.

            Cleaner required to work 10 hours
            each week on Fridays and Saturdays.
            Above average pay.

            Apply by telephone to Ms Rose Smith,
            Cleaning Supervisor, on 01234-751239.
```

Fig. 12. Example of a simple newspaper advertisement.

```
            NOTICE

            TO ALL STAFF

            There will be a meeting of all staff on Tuesday
            5 May 199- to discuss the introduction of new
            time sheets.

            Please come along to the staff rest room at
            1830 hrs. The meeting will last for approximately
            one hour.

            Robert Power
            General Manager

            6 April 199-
```

Fig. 13. Example of a notice to staff.

Memos

A memorandum — memo for short — is a more formal way of passing information from one person to another, or from one department to another within the same organisation. Unlike an informal note a memo is almost always typed and larger organisations usually have their own printed memo paper to use.

A copy of a memo is usually taken for the sender's file. Sometimes NCR (No Carbon Required) paper is used. This consists of several sheets of paper sealed at the top. As you type or print out, the print automatically goes through to all copies. This paper is often used where copies of the same memo have to be sent to different departments. The paper may be in different colours to indicate these various departments.

A memo is similar in many ways to a letter. It is, however, less formal than a normal business letter as the people involved usually know each other. Sometimes such familiarity can lead to entertaining reading if grievances are aired in particularly graphic detail! See figure 14 for an example.

MEMORANDUM

To   Susan Jones

From   Robert Power

Ref   AUT/651

Date   28 March 199-

EXCHANGE OF FURNITURE IN GENERAL OFFICE

I am writing to advise you that Steele & Co will be calling at the beginning of next week, probably on Monday, to change over the chairs and desks.

Perhaps you could make sure that the desks are cleared by Friday afternoon at the latest.

I hope that the new furniture will prove to be successful.

Fig. 14. A simple memo.

COMPILING A REPORT

A report is intended to pass information from a person who has collected it to a person who has asked for this information. Reports in some shape or form are very common in business life. They can cover many subjects and they can be very simple as well as very complex.

Planning your report

Before compiling any report, certain questions should be asked:

What is the purpose of the report?_____

Who is going to read it?_____

How will you obtain the necessary information? _____

How will you present the report?_____

Once you have the answers to these questions clear in your mind you are ready to start preparing your report.

Typical structure of a report

Most reports will contain the following:

● The Title.

● The Introduction — stating what the report is about.

● The Main Body — where all the relevant information is set out, sub-divided into paragraphs as necessary. Make sure you proceed in a logical way, leading the reader on from one point to the next.

Findings

● The Conclusion and any Recommendations — giving definite reasons for both.

● Acknowledgements — if someone has helped you with your report, then it is polite to mention their name at the end. Similarly, if you have used material from books or newspapers, you should list your sources.

● Appendices — for any additional information.

Compiling a report step-by-step

1. Make sure you know the purpose of the report.

2. Decide what the report should aim to achieve.

3. Gather together all the relevant information.

4. Sort the information into logical order.

5. Prepare a first draft of the report.

6. Read and amend where appropriate.

7. Prepare a final copy of the report.

8. Circulate the report as necessary.

Preparing the layout of a report

There are many different ways of presenting a report. The example in figure 15 shows a simple presentation.

DESIGNING A FORM

Uses of forms

Forms have a variety of uses in an office environment. Such uses may include:

●   To set out information in a standard way for colleagues.

●   To record various facts and figures.

●   To show statistical information (*eg* stock records, costings, budgets).

●   To make it easier to analyse information objectively.

●   To help management decision-making.

If an organisation tends to use standard forms, these may be professionally printed, or prepared on the computer and stored, to be reproduced or amended as required.

REPORT ON VISIT BY ROBERT POWER TO PROPOSED
NEW CARAVAN SITE AT BEACHY POINT, NEWTOWN,
DORSET
DATE OF VISIT: Monday 4 May 199-

I met Robin Payne, on site at 0930 hrs. He explained that the
land available extended to 200 acres, which should be sufficient for our needs.

Access
Access did not appear to be a problem. There were three access
roads leading onto the site and all of these joined a main road
within half a mile.

Suitability of land
The entire site was reasonably flat and would need little levell-
ing. There were a number of trees, many of which would have
to stay, but these should not present any problems.

Price
The negotiated price would seem to be a fair one. It would
obviously be a huge commitment to all of us involved, which
must be carefully thought about.

Conclusion and Recommendations
My own conclusion was that the investment would be a good
one. The site seemed absolutely ideal. I would recommend that
everyone gives this matter immediate consideration as other
parties are now interested in purchasing the site too. Please
could I have your decisions by Monday next, 11 May.

Fig. 15. A simple report showing headings and paragraphs.

Designing a form
When designing a form, consider the following:

- The purpose of the form.
- What type of person will use the form.
- The information required on the form.
- The layout of the form.
- The questions to be asked.

When designing any form, the key point to remember is to leave enough space for answers to be inserted. There is nothing more infuriating than trying to fill in a form where insufficient space has been left.

Example: Sally designs a job application form

Sally Avery has been asked by Susan Jones to prepare a form to be used for Job Applications. Look at her first and then her second, amended, attempt.

APPLICATION FOR EMPLOYMENT

Surname . . . . .Forename/s . . . .

Address . . . .

Tel No . . . . Date of Birth . . . .

Schools and Colleges . . . .

. . . .

Qualifications . . . .

. . . .

Present Employment . . . .

Previous Experience . . . .

. . . .

Hobbies and Interests . . . .

Character Reference . . . .

. . . .

. . . .

. . . .

Signed . . . . Date . . . .

Fig. 16. An application form — poor example of layout.

Notes

1. Sally has not allowed enough lines for the form to be properly completed.

2. She should have left an extra space before 'Signed' and 'Date' in case the person signing has a large signature.

3. The main heading would look better in bold type if possible.

APPLICATION FOR EMPLOYMENT

Surname .... Forenames ....

Address ....

....

....

Tel No .... Date of Birth ....

Schools and Colleges ....

....

....

Qualifications ....

....

....

....

....

Present Employment ....

....

....

Hobbies and Interests ....

....

Character Reference ....

....

....

....

Signed .... Date ....

Fig. 17. An application form — better example of layout.

Assignment

Imagine you are Linda Grant, personal assistant to Robert Power. You have been asked to design a form entitled STAFF PERSONAL RECORD FORM. The following headings should be included:

Name/Address/Position/Age/Date Employed/Appraisal Interview Dates/ Days Absent/Comments

USING INVOICES, STATEMENTS AND ORDERS

When a business transaction takes place, many different documents pass between the buyer and seller. The most common documents are explained below:

Enquiry

The buyer will ask the seller for details of the goods available. This enquiry will normally be set out in letter form.

Quotation

The seller sends the necessary details, such as price, quantity, description of goods and date of supply to the buyer, either by letter or on a printed form which may include standard terms and conditions.

Order

If the buyer is satisfied with the quotation, he will place an order for the goods he requires, again either by letter or printed form.

Delivery note

When the goods are delivered the buyer will be asked by the driver to sign a copy of the delivery note to verify that the goods have been received.

Invoice

This is probably the most common business document used. The seller sends a sales invoice to the buyer stating full details of the goods which have been delivered, including the amount of money due and the time given for payment, *eg* 30 days. See fig. 18 for an example.

Credit note

If any goods are returned, the supplier will issue a credit note to the buyer allowing him to use the value of this against future purchases.

Invoice No: 203

Stationery Supplies Ltd
The Street
Bridgeton
West Sussex
BN12 9JU

VAT Reg No 345 689 423

Date: 8 May 199-

To: Seaview Holiday Caravan Park
             Plydmouth
             West Sussex
             BN21 7YH

Your Order: 2091

Terms: 30 days

Cat No	Quality and Description		Price £	Total £
231/TY	12	Boxes of DL Envelopes	10.00	120.00
2341/D	10	Reams A4 Duke Paper	5.00	50.00
2346/Y	1	Box A4 Documents	12.00	12.00
		Sub Total	27.00	182.00
		VAT Total		31.85
		TOTAL		£213.85

E & OE

Fig. 18. A sample invoice.

96

Statement

Usually sent monthly or quarterly. Statements give full details of all transactions which have taken place and been invoiced during the statement period, and the amount now due for payment. Payment should be made when the statement reaches the buyer.

Value Added Tax

Value Added Tax or VAT is a very complicated tax, with an explanation outside the realms of this book. It suffices to say that traders with a turnover over a certain amount per annum must be registered for VAT. This means they usually have to charge their customers VAT on goods they sell, and pay this over to HM Customs and Excise. Theoretically the trader should be able to claim enough VAT back from goods purchased, telephone bills, petrol and so on to break even, but in practice this does not always happen.

E & OE

The seller will often have 'E & OE' printed at the bottom of his business documents. This means 'errors and omissions excepted'. It protects the seller for any error that may have been made in the documentation. For example, if £5.00 appears on an invoice instead of £50.00, the seller is still within his rights to claim the full £50.00 from the buyer.

PREPARING A CURRICULUM VITAE FOR JOB HUNTING

'Curriculum Vitae' is Latin for 'the course of a life' and is often shortened to CV. It is a list of your personal details and employment skills and experience, and it should contain everything relevant to job hunting.

The main aim of a CV is to lead to the offer of an interview. It will therefore need to be clearly and carefully displayed to attract the attention of a prospective employer, who probably has hundreds or even thousands of applications to sift through.

Selecting the right information

It may be a good idea to include certain information when applying for one particular job which you might want to leave out when applying for a different job. For example if applying for a job as a nanny, you could mention the fact that you spent a lot of time helping with your own baby brother, but for a job working in a sales office, this information would be somewhat irrelevant!

CURRICULUM VITAE

NAME	Rita Shirley Payne
ADDRESS	37 Sea Road Plydmouth West Sussex BN14 3RG
TELEPHONE NUMBER	01234-764312
DATE OF BIRTH	4 June 1962
NATIONALITY	British
MARITAL STATUS	Married

EDUCATION

	St John's High School	1973-1978
	Wyndmouth College	1978-1980

QUALIFICATIONS

GCE 'O' Levels:

English Language	Grade A	1978
Mathematics	Grade B	1978
French	Grade B	1978
German	Grade B	1978
Spanish	Grade B	1978
Biology	Grade C	1978

GCE 'A' Levels

English	Grade A	1980
French	Grade A	1980
German	Grade A	1980

PRESENT EMPLOYER	Seaview Holiday Caravan Park Plydmouth West Sussex	1985-date
PRESENT POSITION	Children's Entertainer	
PREVIOUS EXPERIENCE	Children's Entertainer for Chiltern Cruises	1980-1985
OTHER RELEVANT INFORMATION	Clean Driving Licence	
HOBBIES AND INTERESTS	Tennis, Squash, Reading, Walking	
REFEREES	On request	

Fig.19. A sample Curriculum Vitae (CV).

Putting things into correct order

When listing examination results make sure they are shown in chronological (date) order. Employment details should start with your present or most recent job listed first. Any previous experience can follow on afterwards.

At first your CV will probably go on one page. When you have gained more experience and more past employers to list, it may well go onto a second page.

The accompanying letter

Always send a short accompanying letter with a CV. This letter should give details of the job you are applying for and your reasons for doing so. Say why you think you would be suitable but do not repeat information given in your CV.

ASSIGNMENTS

For these assignments imagine you are Susan Jones, office manager.

1. Design a form suitable for all staff wishing to apply for annual holiday leave.

2. Prepare a memo to send to Robert Power. Give the memo the heading 'Holiday Leave Forms'. Enclose a copy of your form and ask for his comments.

CHECKLIST

With all types of written communication:

● Decide on the **purpose** of the communication.

● Decide what you hope to **achieve**.

● Gather all the relevant **information**.

● **Sort** the information into a logical order.

● Make sure the information is **accurate**.

● Prepare a rough **draft** first.

- **Read** the draft through carefully.

- **Amend** where necessary, then produce the final copy.

- **Check** once more for errors or inaccuracies.

POINTS FOR DISCUSSION

1. What would be the differences between using a typewriter and using a word processing program for your daily office correspondence? Which would you prefer to use and why?

2. What are the most important points to remember when writing a business letter?

3. Work with a partner. Each of you sets out in draft form your CV. Discuss with each other whether the content of each is correct and then prepare final copies.

How to Write a Report

John Bowden

Written by an experienced manager and staff trainer, this well-presented handbook provides a very clear step-by-step framework for every individual, whether dealing with professional advisers, banks, customers, clients, suppliers or junior or senior staff. Contents: Preparation and planning. Collecting and handling information. Writing the report. Improving your thinking. Improving presentation. Achieving a good writing style. Making effective use of English. Illustrations. Choosing paper, covers and binding. Appendices, glossary, index. John Bowden BSc(Econ) MSc has long experience both as a professional manager in industry, and as a Senior Lecturer running numerous courses in accountancy, auditing, and effective communication, up to senior management level.

£7.99, 160pp illus. 1 85703 091 5. 2nd edition. Please add postage & packing (UK £1 per copy, Europe £2 per copy, World £3 per copy airmail).

How To Books Ltd, Plymbridge House, Estover Road, Plymouth PL6 7PZ, United Kingdom. Tel: (01752) 695745. Fax: (01752) 695699. Telex: 45635.

Credit card orders may be faxed or phoned.

8
How to Store and
Present Information

We need to use all kinds of information at work, and when it is not being communicated from one person to another, it may need to be stored in a place from which it can easily be retrieved. In this chapter we will discuss:

- why do we need to store information?

- deciding how to store it

- setting up a new manual filing system

- using an existing manual filing system

- using microfilm and electronic filing systems

- finding and presenting information

- reproducing information

WHY DO WE NEED TO STORE INFORMATION?

We need to store information in order for it to be readily available when required. If important documents are lost, time is wasted in searching for them. If they cannot be found, communication breaks down and a chain of serious problems can result. In the business world this means that information needs to be put in some sort of storage system where it can be located and retrieved easily.

DECIDING HOW TO STORE IT

There are three main ways of storing information, using:

- a manual filing system

- a microfilm filing system

- an electronic or computerised system.

  Whichever way is chosen, the main aims should be

(a) to keep the system as simple as possible, so that everyone can use it

(b) to file regularly so that files are kept up to date, and

(c) to protect documents from damage.

Which storage system?

When deciding which system to use, keep the following in mind:

- The system must be **quick and simple** to operate.

- The files should be easily **accessible**.

- The system should be **suitable** for the type of business documents to be placed in it.

- The system should be capable of **expansion**.

- The system should be capable of **safeguarding** documents, including confidential information.

SETTING UP A NEW MANUAL FILING SYSTEM

A manual filing system means one in which papers are stored by hand in filing cabinets, in folders, on shelves, in box files, lever arch files *etc*.

Centralised or departmental filing?

With a centralised filing system, all the files for the whole organisation are stored in one place, which is usually manned by specialised staff.

Advantages of a centralised system
- All the files are kept together.

- Specialised staff are likely to be more efficient.

- A standardised system will be used throughout.

- Duplication of filing equipment is reduced.

- Documents are accessible to all departments all the time.

With a departmentalised filing system, each department has its own files which everyone in that department has access to.

Advantages of a departmental system
- The files are more readily available to each department.

- Different filing systems can be adapted for different departments.

- More suitable for confidential files.

- A smaller system can be easier to operate.

- Departmental staff, who know their department well, will be expert at filing their own papers.

Once the decision has been taken on where to locate the files, the actual equipment to be used is the next point to consider.

Vertical or lateral filing?

The vertical method is the most popular way of filing. The files are suspended in an upright position in drawers of metal filing cabinets. The contents of the files are listed on strips which are placed on the top edge of each file. The documents are kept clean and dust-free and are easily accessible. Filing cabinets, although expensive to buy and equip, last for many years and are very easy to use.

Care should be taken when opening the drawers of filing cabinets. If you pull open a fully loaded top drawer too suddenly, or open more than one drawer at a time, there is a chance that the cabinet will tip over.

With lateral filing the files are suspended from rails in horizontal rows on racks or shelves, rather like books on a bookshelf. Where space is limited lateral filing is a good idea, as there are no filing drawers to open and the shelves or racks can be built right up to the ceiling if necessary.

One of the main disadvantages of this system, however, is that usually the files are not protected from dust and dirt and high shelves can pose problems for the staff involved in getting the files down.

Alphabetical or numerical filing

The final decision to make is whether to file the documents in alphabetical order, by number, or maybe a combination of both.

The alphabetical system is quick and simple to operate. All staff, including temps, can quickly learn what to do. Files should be placed in correct alphabetical order according to organisation name or, if there is not an organisation name, the individual name. Occasionally, for instance in a planning office, files may be placed alphabetically according to road, town or county, or they may be grouped by subject, *eg* static caravans, tourers, motorhomes, and tents.

Examples of alphabetical order

Private names	*Company names*
A Bruce	Auto Motors Ltd
B C Downland	Deangate Hospital
J Smith	Red Lion Hotel
A Whyle	Whitegate Furnishers

Geographical	*Subject*
Leicester	Advertising
London	Personnel
Manchester	Sales

Numerical filing

With numerical order, each name, document or folder is given a number and they are then placed in consecutive number order. Often this system incorporates an index where an alphabetical list is kept too in case the number of the required file is not known.

The numerical system is easily capable of expansion as numbers can go on for ever, but it can be more complicated to operate than the alphabetical system, particularly if a separate index is used.

Assignment

Put the following files of caravan owners into the correct alphabetical order, ready for filing. Where full first names are shown, abbreviate to initials.

Mr and Mrs A C Brown	Mr and Mrs MacJones
Mr T P Andrews	Mr S Platt
Mr and Mrs J Smith	Mr and Mrs K Prior
Mrs Rose James	Richard and Karen Moore
Mr and Mrs H Harry	Mr P and Mrs A Carr
Mr John Jones	Mrs Sheila Black
Mr and Mrs McPherson	Mr and Mrs St John
Mr Simon Westgate	Mrs Avril Plant

USING AN ESTABLISHED MANUAL FILING SYSTEM

When using an existing filing system, you will first of all need to familiarise yourself with that system and how it works.

Effective filing

There are then a few basic tips to remember for successful filing:

● Make sure that the documents have been released for filing.

● Sort and group the documents before starting to file.

● Place the documents carefully in the file so that they do not crease or become tatty.

● Ensure that the correct documents are placed in the correct file.

● Never attach paper clips to documents being placed in a file as these clips can become loose or tangled up with other documents. Staple papers together if necessary.

● It is best to arrange the documents within a file in date order, so that the most recent is on top, but check first to make sure this is correct policy.

● 'Thin out' bulky files from time to time, but only when you have authority to do so.

● Lock the filing cabinets if you are asked to do so.

● File daily so that the system is always up to date.

USING MICROFILM AND ELECTRONIC FILING SYSTEMS

The problem faced by many organisations is lack of space to store the enormous number of business documents they need to keep. One of the best ways of reducing this space is by the use of microfilming.

Microfilming

Microfilming is the filing of documents that have been photographed, developed on film in greatly reduced size and printed on plastic strips or cards. An A4 sheet of information can be reduced to a tiny size. If the document needs to be read, a viewfinder is used to enlarge the image on the screen. If a hard copy (paper copy) is required, the enlarged image can be reproduced.

Electronic filing

Electronic systems of filing, such as word processors and computers, enable documents to be filed on a computer storage medium. There are many ways of storing information on computers; technology is advancing all the time.

Common ways of storing documents on microcomputers include the use of floppy and hard disks.

- A **floppy disk** is portable; in other words it is removed from the machine, and has to be inserted to call up files on it;

- the **hard disk** is the computer's built in storage facility; files on the hard disk can be accessed at any time.

Example

Sally Avery, the WP operator, is sending a letter to a customer. As she keys the letter in on her microcomputer, it will be displayed on the screen. She can make as many alterations, additions, and deletions as she likes before printing the letter out.

The hard (paper) copy of the letter can be shown to Susan Jones and if necessary amended on the screen and printed out once more. The final version of Sally's letter can then be stored on a floppy disk along with other documents.

If Sally needs this or any other document in the future, she can insert the appropriate disk, call up the file, and view the document on the screen again. Hard copies can be printed out at any time.

FINDING AND PRESENTING INFORMATION

In any organisation, information needs to be found ('accessed') every working day. The filing system is the place to begin your search for information.

When removing a file from a manual filing system, make sure you always fill in an **absent card**. On this card you should record the date taken, the file number or name, and your name. When you return the file you should fill in the date returned. That way, if someone else needs the file in a hurry they will know who to come to.

Keeping a 'bring forward' file
Business correspondence often needs to be acted upon, not just filed away. In these circumstances a 'bring forward' file can be very useful.

A bring forward file usually contains 12 'pockets', one for each month of the year. In addition, there should be 31 pockets to cater for each day of the current month. It is a good idea to keep a diary note of correspondence in the bring forward file; you can then check your diary each day to see if any action is needed.

Example: the advance ballroom booking
A letter comes in to Robert Power. It is about a dance to be arranged in the Park Ballroom one weekend during the winter. The letter is dated 12 June 199- and in it, Mr Rover, the sender, asks Robert to contact him again at the end of August. Robert asks Linda Grant, his personal assistant, to look after the letter until needed.

Linda has a bring forward file and she places the letter in the August compartment. She then makes a diary note for 20 August, to remind her to look for the letter.

Maintaining your files
Always be careful when handling files. Do not change the order of the documents, unless they were incorrectly filed in the first place. Take care not to drop anything out of files. Return files as promptly as possible.

If you are obtaining a file for someone else and you think it could be needed elsewhere, or the person concerned is not very careful with papers, then, with that person's approval, it could be a good idea to photocopy the relevant pages and use these, so that the file itself can be returned to the main filing system.

Information not 'on file'

Not all information is kept in a filing system. Specialist technical books and reference books will also be found within business organisations. Important reference books include

- a good dictionary

- an encyclopedia

- a thesaurus

- the Royal Mail Guide

- telephone directories

- maps and travel information.

In addition, a great deal of information is available through electronic databases such as Ceefax, Prestel and Oracle.

REPRODUCING INFORMATION

Paper documents can be reproduced using a photocopying machine or a fax machine. With sophisticated electronic photocopiers, perfect copies can be made, both in black and white and often in colour too.

Information stored on microfilm or computer disk can easily be accessed as explained in the section **MICROFILM AND ELEC-TRONIC FILING SYSTEMS** above, and copies can be made as necessary.

ASSIGNMENTS

For these assignments imagine you are Pat Thain, secretary to Jim Bruce, sales manager.

1. Jim has asked you to set up a new filing system for Sales. The system is to house all existing customers, potential customers, and correspondence from various caravan dealers and manufacturers. You have a spare room available to house the files.

    (a) Would you choose a vertical or lateral system?
    (b) What equipment would you need?

(c)   How would you operate the system, *ie* using alphabetical or numerical filing?

Give the reasons for your choices.

2.   Jim needs to take a file on a business trip. You think you may need it while he is away. How could you get round this problem?

CHECKLIST

Setting up the filing system

● Choose a system that will cope with your needs.

● Make sure it will be quick and simple to operate.

● Think about security for confidential documents.

Using the filing system

● Never file documents until they are finished with.

● Keep filing up to date.

● File documents in the correct place.

● If removing a file fill in an absent card.

● Keep a bring forward file for documents needing action in the future.

● Always remember, efficient filing means an efficient organisation.

POINTS FOR DISCUSSION

1.   Why is it so important to operate an effective filing system? Give five reasons.

2.   What are the advantages and disadvantages of centralised filing and departmental filing?

3.   Design a simple 'absent card' to be put in place of a file when it is removed from the filing system.

9
How to Deal with
Travel and Meetings

People often communicate best when meeting face to face, so an important aspect of communication skills at work is to organise meetings, and any necessary travel arrangements for those meetings.

Travel
- choosing between road, rail and air travel

- planning trips abroad

- preparing an itinerary.

Meetings
- meetings: formal or informal

- arranging dates, times, places and programmes

- attending meetings

- making notes at meetings

- understanding terms used at meetings.

It is very likely that at some time or other in your working life you may have to arrange business travel either for yourself or for your employer. This may involve travelling in this country or abroad.

ROAD, RAIL OR AIR TRAVEL?

There are several ways of travelling around the country. These include travel by car and travel by train. In addition, many places are now accessible by air. It is not always easy to decide which form of transport to take.

Points to consider
Here are a few points to think about:

- The distance involved — is the destination many miles away, or just a few?

- The time available — flying is obviously much quicker for long distances, providing your place of work and your destination are both near an airport.

- The cost of the journey. Travelling by car usually works out the cheapest, followed by rail and then air.

- Preference. If you or your employer hate travelling by any form of public transport, then driving would be the best answer. In addition, many people are terrified of flying, and would not consider taking a plane if they can possibly avoid it.

Reference sources to help you
There are various reference sources available. These include:

- Maps and guides available from motoring organisations such as the AA and RAC.

- The *ABC Rail Guide* and various localised rail timetables.

- The *ABC World Airways Guide*.

PLANNING TRIPS ABROAD

In recent years contact with foreign colleagues has increased dramatically due to an increase in global trading. As a result, many staff are now regularly required to travel abroad, sometimes for long trips and sometimes just for the day.

It helps tremendously if business trips abroad can be planned well in advance. Costs can be kept down, and the organisation should be able to get better value from the trip if it is not planned in a hectic rush.

What needs to be arranged
Apart from booking the method of transport, a number of other arrangements have to be made:

- Arrange travel tickets and hotel accommodation.

- Check that passports and visas are up to date.

- Make sure that everyone travelling is aware of vaccination requirements.

- Arrange for insurance cover.

- Take care of currency requirements and travellers cheques.

- Arrange car hire if necessary.

- Provide back-up information in the way of maps and guides.

- Organise a typed itinerary for the visit.

- Make sure that you or your employer can be contacted in an
emergency.

Documents and papers to take

When the visit actually takes place, you or your employer must remember to take the following:

- passports, tickets and other travel documentation

- any confirmation of hotel accommodation

- currency, travellers cheques and credit cards

- vaccination certificates (if appropriate)

- copy of the typed itinerary

- maps and guides of the area to be visited

- first aid and any necessary medication

- address book and stationery for notes and messages

- relevant files and documents for business meetings

Reference sources for travel abroad include:

- AA and RAC publish maps and guides for other countries

- the *ABC Rail Guide* (parts of Europe)

- *ABC Air/Rail Europe* and *Middle East Guide*

- *ABC World Airways Guide*

Probably the best help of all when planning a trip abroad is to speak to your local travel agency. They are the experts and will plan everything to do with travel, accommodation, currency and car hire, as well as advise on passport and visa requirements, whether vaccinations are necessary and anything else remotely connected with the visit.

Planning an overseas business trip step-by-step

1. Check the exact location(s) of the meeting(s) to be held.

2. Decide on date of departure and duration of stay.

3. Arrange transport and accommodation for the visit, and car hire if needed. (Or make these arrangements through a travel agent.)

4. Check whether passports and/or visas are required.

5. Obtain foreign currency and travellers' cheques.

6. Prepare an itinerary (see below).

7. At least a day before departure, finally check that all necessary documentation and luggage is ready.

8. Refer to itinerary during trip and keep in touch with colleagues back home.

PREPARING AN ITINERARY

An itinerary is a list or programme of places a person is due to visit on a trip. It should be clear and easy to read and everyone who needs to know the person's whereabouts will require a copy. An itinerary should be planned in date and time order. It should allow for time differences between our country and countries abroad when organising the schedule. Remember also to allow for travelling between appointments. Someone cannot realistically be expected to be in Rome in the morning and Paris at lunchtime!

If an itinerary is short it can be produced on a card, small enough to fit in a pocket. If, however, it is long and complicated, use ordinary A4 paper. The itinerary can then be placed in a clear plastic folder to keep it clean.

Example of an itinerary

PROPOSED VISIT BY ROBERT POWER TO NEW CARAVAN SITE AT BEACHY POINT, NEWTOWN, DORSET, ON MONDAY 18TH JULY 199-

0800	hrs	Meet with John Wright at Seaview Reception.
0830	hrs	John and Robert to depart for Beachy Point by car.
1030	hrs	Arrive at Beachy Point. Coffee at Hotel Nelson, opposite the site.
1100	hrs	Meet with Tom Sharpe, Site Foreman.
1300	hrs	Lunch at Hotel Nelson with Peter Spall, the Site Manager, to discuss opening dates.
1500	hrs	Depart Beachy Point for return drive to Seaview.
1700	hrs	Arrive back at Seaview. Robert and John to dine in Restaurant at approximately 1800 hrs, to discuss the day's events.

Assignment

Draw up an itinerary for Jim to use when he visits Beachy Point on Tuesday 12 September to talk to Peter Spall about caravan sales and the appoint of a sales manager at the new site. They will discuss all this over lunch at 1300 hrs in the Nelson Hotel. Jim expects to arrive about 1100 hrs and depart at 1600 hrs. In between he needs to have a tour of the new site and take a drive to Country Caravans who have a branch in nearby Weymouth.

MEETINGS: FORMAL OR INFORMAL?

An informal meeting is one where a group of people meet to exchange ideas or information in an unofficial or casual way. No official notes are taken and the meeting is really no more than a glorified 'chat' between colleagues.

A formal meeting, on the other hand, is **documented** before, during and after it takes place. It may be a committee meeting, an annual general meeting for shareholders or just a company meeting held from time to time. Some meetings may be more formal than others, particularly annual general meetings, according to the constitution of the organisation in question.

ARRANGING DATES, TIMES, PLACES AND PROGRAMMES

Before a formal meeting takes place, a **Notice of Meeting** is sent out to those entitled to attend. This states the date, time and the place where the meeting is to be held.

The **Agenda** or programme is either combined with the Notice of Meeting, or sent separately at a later date. The Agenda lists in a logical order the items to be discussed. Both of these documents will usually be prepared by the Secretary in conjunction with the Chairperson, who will be presiding over the meeting.

A Chairperson's Agenda can be different in appearance, in that it often has a wide right hand margin for the Chairperson to make notes as the meeting proceeds.

An example of a combined Notice and Agenda is shown in figure 20.

ATTENDING THE MEETING

Meetings can interesting or dull, according to who attends them and how they are conducted. Some meetings drag on and on, with no obvious conclusions being reached, and with everyone sitting around looking half asleep. Other meetings, briskly run by an efficient chairperson, achieve their aims and serve a very useful purpose.

Benefits of attending a meeting
Whatever the type of meeting, it is possible for you to benefit by:

● learning more about the colleagues you are with

Fig. 20. Example of a combined notice and agenda for a meeting.

- listening to the thoughts and opinions of others

- communicating with your colleagues, expressing your own ideas

- feeling part of a 'team'.

Communication skills for meetings

In order to be able to communicate effectively at a meeting you must be able to:

- show consideration and tolerance for others.

- speak clearly and use words that everyone will understand.

- speak at the appropriate time, and not when someone else is already speaking.

- understand that your views will not necessarily be the same as everyone else's. Be prepared to compromise.

Always take the opportunity to speak at a meeting. Your silent views are of no use to anyone. Do not force yourself on the others, but rather make your points in a steady and easy manner, showing that you are not out to make war, merely to state your case.

A successful meeting is one where everyone leaves feeling confident that they know exactly what is going to happen next, and who is going to be responsible for 'actioning' the points raised.

MAKING NOTES AT THE MEETING

It is important for notes to be taken at formal meetings. These notes are known as **minutes**. It is usually, although not always, the secretary who takes down the minutes as the meeting progresses. These notes are not normally verbatim (word for word), but should contain

- relevant points of discussion

- all resolutions

- all recommendations.

After the meeting these notes will be used to prepare a rough draft of the minutes, and then, after consultation with the chairperson, the final copy will be produced.

The minute book

Most organisations will have their own format for the display of minutes and this format should be strictly adhered to. The minutes will often be placed in a **minute book** or a special file where, following on from previous minutes, they provide a permanent record, so consistency is necessary.

Remaining objective

If you are ever involved with taking notes at a meeting it is most important not to let your own personal feelings and prejudices get in the way of your note taking. Your account of the meeting should be totally unbiased.

There are several different ways of setting out minutes. The example on page 118 gives one suggestion. The action column over on the right hand side gives the initials of the personnel who are to take action on the various subjects discussed.

SEAVIEW HOLIDAY CARAVAN PARK

Minutes of the Meeting of the Management Team held in The Oasis Club on Monday 10 September 199- at 1900 hrs.

PRESENT

Robert Power (Chairperson)
Linda Grant (Secretary)
Susan Jones
Jim Bruce
Ron Green
James Taylor
Rose Smith

		ACTION
APOLOGIES FOR ABSENCE	Everyone was present at the meeting.	
MINUTES OF LAST MEETING	The Minutes of the last meeting on 10 July were read and approved as a correct record.	
MATTERS ARISING OUT OF THE MINUTES	There were no matters arising out of the minutes.	
REPORT ON BEACHY HEAD SITE	Robert reported on his visit to Beachy Head on 18 July. He had met both Tom Sharpe, the Site Foreman and Peter Spall the Site Manager. Good progress was being made and the site should be completed by the Spring of 199-. Robert to speak to Tom again about a definite date.	RP
REPORT ON MAINS CONNECTIONS FOR NEXT YEAR	Ron Green reported that plans were going ahead for 30 more mains plots on the north side of the park. He was waiting a date for the work to begin. Robert Power asked him to chase.	RG
ANY OTHER BUSINESS	There was no other business.	
DATE OF NEXT MEETING	It was agreed that the date of next meeting would be 12 November 199-.	

Fig. 21. Example of minutes of meeting.

TERMS COMMONLY USED AT MEETINGS

There are certain standard terms that are often used at meetings and
it is a good idea to become familiar with them before attending a
meeting for the first time.

Abstain
To refrain from voting.

Ad hoc
This usually refers to a committee specially appointed to carry out a
specific task (rather than a permanent or 'standing' committee).

Address the chair
This means that those wishing to speak must do so by speaking to
the person in the chair, *ie* the chairperson, rather than carrying on
conversations between themselves.

Adjournment
A decision taken to adjourn the meeting, for example for a lunch
break.

Amendment
This is a proposal to alter a **motion** (see below). It must be proposed, seconded and voted on before a decision is taken.

Any other business
The 'any other business' time in a meeting gives an opportunity for
those present to discuss items other than those listed under separate
headings. It is often abbreviated to 'AOB'.

Ballot
Method of voting by means of a voting paper.

Carried
A motion that has been agreed.

Casting vote
If voting on a motion is equal, the chairperson may have the power
to cast his or her vote, thus making the decision.

Committee
A group of people who meet to make decisions on behalf of an organisation.

Delegate, a
Someone who represents a group of people and gives their views.

In camera
A meeting in private, one not open to the public.

Lie on the table
This is when a document is not to be acted on and it is said to 'lie on the table'.

Majority
This means the number of votes necessary to carry a motion.

Motion
A proposal put forward at a meeting is known as a **motion**. When a motion is put forward it is known as a **question**. If it is passed it is known as a **resolution**. It is usually necessary to propose and second a motion before it can be discussed.

No confidence
If those present at a meeting are not happy with the actions of their chairperson, they can take a vote of 'no confidence'. If this is passed, the chairperson must vacate the chair in favour of another nominated person.

Postponement
This is the action taken to put off a meeting to a later date.

Proxy vote
A person who cannot attend a meeting can ask someone else to vote on his or her behalf. The person is known as a **proxy** and the vote is called a **proxy vote**.

Quorum
With most formal meetings a certain minimum number of people must be present before the meeting can take place. This number is known as a quorum.

Resolution
A motion passed at a meeting.

Unanimous
All of one mind — a decision taken with the approval of every person at the meeting.

ASSIGNMENTS

For these assignments imagine you are Linda Grant, personal assistant to Robert Power.

1. Prepare the Notice and Agenda for the meeting to be held on 12 November 199-. The Agenda will be the same as the last one, but should have one extra heading: CHRISTMAS ARRANGEMENTS

2. Prepare a Travel Itinerary for Robert to visit France in February. He will be flying from Gatwick to Charles de Gaulle Airport in Paris. His flight out is BY325 on 8 February at 1000 hrs. His return flight is BY357 on 13 February at 1300 hrs. He will be staying at Hotel de Paris. He will be visiting the following sites:
    CHATEAU DE LA FONTAINE – NOYAN – 9 Feb
    CAMPING LE ROYAL – CHANTILLY – 10 Feb
    CAMPING DE KERLUT – SENS – 12 Feb

    Apart from that his time is free. Allow 1000 hrs to 1300 hrs for each site.

CHECKLIST

Travel
- Decide on method of transport and accommodation.

- Check on passports, visas, insurance.

- Arrange currency and travellers cheques.

- Arrange car hire if necessary.

●   Prepare an itinerary.

●   Remember that travel agents can help.

Meetings
●   Make sure you know the purpose of the Notice, Agenda and Minutes of a Meeting.

●   Speak clearly and at the appropriate time when attending a meeting.

●   Be prepared to listen to others.

●   Become familiar with the terms used at meetings.

POINTS FOR DISCUSSION

1.   What method of travel would you choose to go from London to Scotland to attend a business meeting? You have two days free. The meeting is in the afternoon of the first day. State the reasons for your decision.

2.   What is the purpose of an Agenda? Name three headings that almost always appear on an Agenda.

3.   Draft a Notice and Agenda for a meeting of the directors of a company known as Apsley Leisure Ltd. The meeting is to be held on 5 July 199-, at 1500 hrs, in the Apsley Suite. Items for discussion: New Sports Centre, Completion of Squash Courts, Any Other Business, Apologies, Mins of last Meeting, Matters arising out of Mins, Date of next Meeting — 6 August 199-, same time.

10
How to Use
Charts and Graphs

In this chapter we will see how charts and graphs can be helpful to us in communicating with colleagues, customers, suppliers and others at work. In particular we will discuss how and when to use the following:

- a table

- a flow chart

- a bar graph

- a line graph

- a pictogram

- a pie chart

- an organisation chart

- an information map or information tree.

HOW CHARTS AND GRAPHS CAN HELP US

Communication in organisations largely means presenting facts and information so that decisions can be made. A lot of these facts are in the form of statistics. When these statistics are presented as text they can become very confusing and difficult to understand.

By using charts and graphs, along with the more traditional written and spoken communication, much of this statistical information can be presented separately — in a way that is easy to understand.

Example
Staff holiday dates at Seaview have always been written in the office

123

diary. One Monday morning Susan Jones realises that Patsy has not arrived. She rings Patsy's number, but there is no reply. At coffee time, Molly happens to open the diary and sees Patsy's holiday written in there.

Susan makes a decision there and then. She purchases a year planner and marks all the holidays clearly on it, with each member of staff shown in a different colour. She then places the year planner in a prominent position on the office wall. As a result, holidays are no longer forgotten and Susan can see at a glance who is away when.

USING A TABLE

A table is a type of chart, arranged systematically in columns. Tables are very good for displaying material containing columns of figures.

Tables can be ruled or unruled. Examples are shown in figures 22 and 23.

SEAVIEW HOLIDAY CARAVAN PARK

OVERTIME PAID TO CLEANERS 7-27 JULY INCLUSIVE

	w/c 7 July £	w/c 14 July £	w/c 21 July £
Avril	10.00	15.00	10.00
Sheila	7.50	15.00	12.50
Lynn	–	–	–
June	12.50	12.50	10.00
Carol	10.00	7.50	7.50
TOTAL	40.00	50.00	40.00

Fig. 22. Example of a table showing overtime pay.

NUMBER OF PLOTS AT SEAVIEW TO BE CONVERTED TO MAINS					
YEAR	AREA A	AREA B	AREA C	AREA D	TOTAL PLOTS
1990	10	15	–	–	25
1991	15	10	15	15	55
1992	10	10	20	20	60
1993	15	20	20	20	70
TOTAL NUMBER OF PLOTS OVER 4 YEARS = 210					

Figure 23. Example of a table showing caravan plots
converted to mains electricity.

Points to remember when preparing a table

● Decide on any necessary sub-headings.

● Allow for ruling where necessary. The ruling can be hand-drawn or produced on the typewriter/computer.

● Check all figures carefully to make sure they tally.

● Leave an equal space between columns.

USING A FLOW CHART

Flow charts show the flow or sequence of events of something. They are very often used for computer programming, but they can also be used to show different procedures carried out at work. An example of a simple flow chart is given in figure 24, and another is shown on page 140. Boxes can be drawn round the text if preferred.

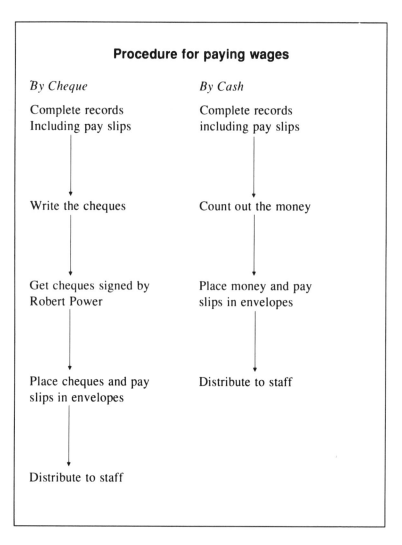

Procedure for paying wages

By Cheque

Complete records
Including pay slips

↓

Write the cheques

↓

Get cheques signed by
Robert Power

↓

Place cheques and pay
slips in envelopes

↓

Distribute to staff

By Cash

Complete records
including pay slips

↓

Count out the money

↓

Place money and pay
slips in envelopes

↓

Distribute to staff

Fig. 24. Flow chart showing how wages are paid.

USING A BAR GRAPH

Bar graphs are a very effective way of displaying information. They are particularly useful for giving a quick comparison of quantities of goods or sums of money. Each bar is separate from the next, unlike a histogram where the bars join on to one another.

The following example shows how a tabulation can be converted into a bar graph, making it much simpler to interpret the facts. The finished bar graph is shown in fig. 25.

Example: data for a bar graph

Monthly Sales of Caravan Jan-June 199-

	NEW	USED	AGENCY
£	£	£	
January	15,000	20,000	10,000
February	10,000	30,000	20,000
March	25,000	20,000	10,000
April	30,000	10,000	30,000
May	20,000	15,000	15,000
June	30,000	20,000	30,000

MONTHLY SALES OF CARAVANS JAN-JUNE 199-

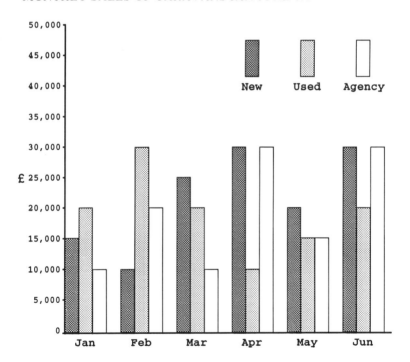

Fig. 25. Example of a bar graph to show monthly caravan sales. Notes:

1. The vertical line on the left represents sums of money ranging from 0 to £50,000. 10mm = £5,000.
2. The horizontal line shows the months, each category side by side.
3. The key is shown on the graph.

USING A LINE GRAPH

The same information could be shown on a line graph, as in the example below.

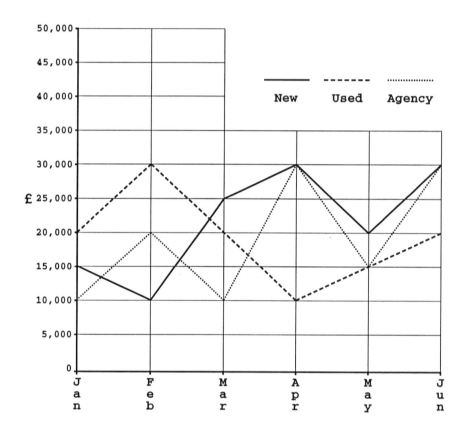

Fig. 26. Example of a line graph to show monthly caravan sales, using the data on page 127. Notes:

1. The vertical line on the left represents sums of money ranging from 0 to £50,000. 10mm = £5,000.

2. The horizontal line shows the months, each category occupying 20mm.

3. The key is shown on the graph.

USING A PICTOGRAM

A pictogram is similar to a bar graph, except that instead of bars, the subject itself is represented by picture symbols as in the example below. It is very good for showing comparisons, but it should be remembered that only a limited amount of information can be shown in this way.

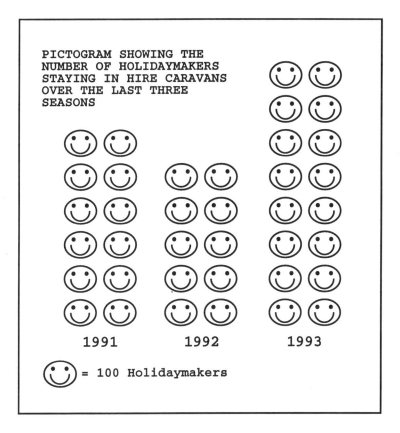

Fig. 27. Example of a pictogram to show holidaymakers in caravans per year. Notes:

1991 = 1,200 holidaymakers.
1992 = 1,000 holidaymakers.
1993 = 1,600 holidaymakers.

USING A PIE CHART

A pie chart, formed by a circle, is a very useful way to show information. The circle is divided into segments, each one representing a percentage of the whole. The main disadvantage is that the circle can only be divided into a limited number of segments, otherwise each segment becomes rather 'thin'. The example of a pie chart in fig. 28 shows how the touring fields at Seaview are divided up.

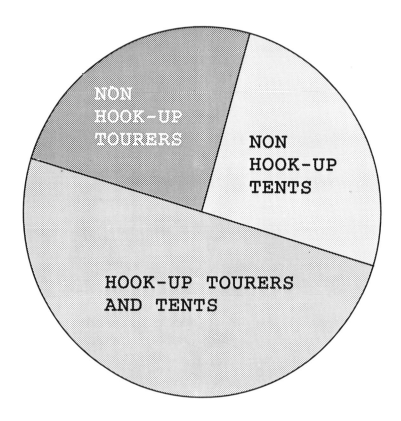

Fig. 28. Example of a pie chart. Notes:

Hook-up tourers and tents:	100	(50%)
Non-hook-up tourers:	50	(25%)
Non-hook-up tents:	50	(25%)
	200	(100%)

USING AN ORGANISATION CHART

An organisation chart shows the organisation or structure of a company. It should show who is in charge of each department and who is responsible to whom. The organisation chart for Seaview Holiday Caravan Park at the beginning of this book gives an example of a typical chart (page 12).

USING AN INFORMATION MAP OR TREE

An information map or tree can look rather like an organisation chart. It does not, however, show the structure of a company. Instead it allows you to show all the items making up a particular subject and their relationship to one another. Often it shows a train of thought and can be a very useful way of note-taking.

An example of a simple information map is given in fig. 29.

PROMOTING SEAVIEW HOLIDAY CARAVAN PARK

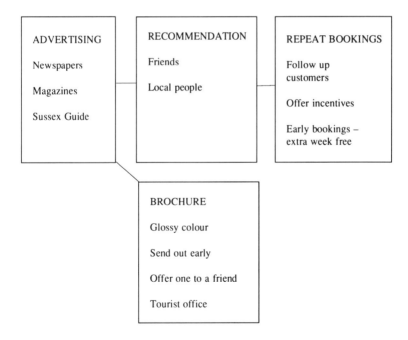

Fig. 29. Example of a simple information map showing types of business promotion.

ASSIGNMENTS

For these assignments imagine you are Linda Grant, personal assistant to Robert Power.

1. Prepare a table containing the following information:

    CABARETS DURING AUGUST
    w/c Sunday 8 Aug, Mon - The Treats, Wed - LouLou,
    Fri - George Brothers
    w/c Sunday 15 Aug, Mon - Sally Tattler, Wed - Coco,
    Fri - April Steven
    w/c Sunday 22 Aug, Mon - LouLou, Wed - Paul and Wendy,
    Fri - The Treats, Mon 30 Aug - George Brothers

    Rule the tabulation horizontally.

2. Prepare a pie chart to show the following information:

    20% of all bookings are new customers
    40% of all bookings have stayed at Seaview before
    20% of all bookings have been recommended by friends
    10% of all bookings have stayed more than five times
    10% of all bookings cancel before their holiday

    Give the chart a suitable heading.

CHECKLIST

● Use charts and graphs to accompany the written or spoken word.

● Keep your examples simple.

● Take care to be accurate when presenting information.

● Remember to add a key where necessary.

POINTS FOR DISCUSSION

1. When is it helpful to use charts and graphs? Give several examples.

2. Prepare an organisation chart for a company called Successful Office Services:

    Molly Hancock, Managing Director. Sue Leech, Office Manager. Jim Bond and Jenny Wright are both responsible to her. They are both Administrative Assistants. Jim has Paula Wells and Jane Steen working for him as WP operators. Sue Leech has a PA called Lindsey Paul. Jenny Wright has two girls under her. Their names are Rhona Payne and Cynthia Bootle. They are both Junior Clerks.

3. How would you show different bars for different subjects in a bar graph if you are preparing the graph in black and white?

11
How to Manage Interviews

In this chapter, we will discuss what an interview is for, and how we use it for communication at work. We will look at both formal and informal interviews. In particular we will discuss

- **being interviewed**
  the job interview
  the appraisal interview
  the disciplinary interview
  the grievance interview

- **interviewing someone else**
  planning an interview
  conducting an interview
  closing an interview.

WHAT IS AN INTERVIEW?

An interview is a spoken exchange of information, usually between two people or between one person and a small group. This exchange of information is generally, although not always, planned in advance. It involves speaking and listening on both sides.

Formal or informal?
Most interviews are formal in nature. There are exceptions, however, such as a boss interviewing his assistant over a pub lunch, perhaps discussing targets for the coming months, or a new project they are about to work on together. Similarly, a company may arrange an informal interview for groups of job applicants prior to the more formal individual interview.

Chance meetings, perhaps in the office canteen or in the corridor, are not really classed as interviews; they are really more of a 'chat'.

Being interviewed

We take a look at four of the most common types of interview.

THE JOB INTERVIEW

This is the type of interview that most of us are familiar with. A job interview can change the course of your entire life and it should be taken very seriously.

Perhaps the first point to make is that you should always accept any offer of a job interview, even if you do not think the job itself is quite what you are looking for. The more interviews you attend, the more experienced and confident you will become.

In advance

If you have been invited to attend for interview, make sure you find out as much as possible about the company beforehand. If you are travelling some distance, do a trial run first, just to check how long it takes. What questions may be put to you? How would you answer them? Prepare some questions of your own to ask the interviewer when requested to do so. Jot them down on a piece of paper, ready to refer to when necessary. Look out any certificates you may have for your qualifications. You will need to take them with you.

On the day

On the day of the interview, allow yourself plenty of time, so that you can arrive just a few minutes early, without looking flustered. Wear smart, comfortable clothes. Take several deep breaths to calm your nerves before entering the office to meet your interviewer. Do not smoke unless invited to do so.

First impressions

Give a good first impression. Smile and say 'Good morning' or 'Good afternoon' as you go in. Your interviewer will probably start with a few pleasantries, perhaps asking about your journey, or commenting on the weather. This is designed to put you at your ease.

The important part

Then will come the main thrust of the interview, and your chance to sell yourself, without appearing false or too cocky. Just act naturally.

An experienced interviewer will soon see through someone who agrees with everything they say, without contributing any original ideas of his or her own.

Never lie at a job interview. Just occasionally the truth can be 'bent' a little, but if you lie the chances are that you will be found out.

Try to answer questions put to you with enthusiasm and confidence. When the time comes for you to ask your own questions, refer to your notes if necessary. This will show that you have given the interview some thought beforehand.

At the end
It is polite to thank the interviewer for their time before you leave the interview room.

Example
Let us take a look at three people being interviewed by Robert Power for a management trainee position at Seaview.

The first interviewee is Rachael, a tall, thin, shy type of girl, lacking in confidence.

The second interviewee is Paul. Paul has bags of self confidence and tries to impress at every opportunity.

The third interviewee is Cher, a young but mature looking girl. Although not particularly attractive in appearance, she dresses well and speaks in a confident manner, thinking carefully before answering questions put to her.

The same question is put to all three interviewees:

'Now, tell me something about your suitability for this job', Robert asks.

Rachael: 'Well, er, I like caravans. My Mum and Dad used to own one and we used to spend all our holidays in it. I really liked being near to the sea. The air is a lot better than in London where I come from.'

Paul: 'Well, I've got just the sort of experience you are looking for. When I was at college I worked at a holiday camp in the summer. The General Manager called me in before I left and told me what an asset I had been. He said he didn't think they would have any management vacancies in the near future, but he thought I could be a real benefit to someone else.'

Cher: 'When I read the job description you sent to me, I thought the position sounded very interesting. My business studies diploma should give me the necessary academic qualifications for the job and I like to think that given the chance I could become a successful member of your management team.'

I'm sure you can come to your own conclusions on who made the best impression, but let's look at why.

Rachael answered the question put to her in a totally irrelevant way. Paul came over as brash, self-opinionated and certainly not a credit to anyone. It was obvious that the holiday camp he had worked at during the holidays would never consider taking him on as a permanent member of staff. Cher, on the other hand, came over as a quietly confident young lady, eager to please and sure of her capabilities.

Let's try another question from Robert.

'What are your main interests?'

Rachael: 'I like dressmaking and I watch quite a lot of television. I like reading too — romances mostly.'

Paul: 'I read a lot, especially management books. I like to travel too. Mind you, I've been to most places now. Russia, China, America — all over really.'

Cher: 'My main hobby is horseriding. I am also secretary at the local Young Farmers Club. This involves attending meetings, taking minutes, dealing with all the correspondence and helping to arrange the various events.'

Rachael's answer is just plain boring. Paul sounds as though he has done it all already, so a job in a seaside caravan park is not likely to satisfy him for long. Once again Cher scores the most points. She has a hobby which is important to her, horseriding, but she also has established some business experience in her role as Young Farmers Club secretary.

These examples will show the importance of answering the questions put to you in a way that will impress and interest the interviewer.

Example of a successful job interview

Mrs Susan Prior is being interviewed by Rose Smith for the position of cleaner. Susan desperately needs the job and is determined to try her hardest to impress. The interview goes as follows:

'Mrs Prior, good morning, do come in.' Rose welcomes her into the room. 'Take a seat. How was your journey here this morning?'

'Thank you. Good morning, Mrs Smith. Actually I only live about a mile away, so I came on my bike,' Susan replies, settling down on the chair offered to her.

'Oh good. No problems about travelling then.' Rose makes a note on her interview file. 'Susan, why have you applied for this position with us, and what makes you think you are what we are looking for?'

(Rose has an application form in front of her which shows that on paper at least Susan is very suitable for the position.)

Susan swallows hard and thinks carefully before answering. 'Well, I am looking for a part-time job that I can manage along with the family, and the Seaview is well known to me. I worked here many years ago when the children were small and it was always a very friendly place. I have many years' experience as a cleaner and have recently been working in private houses, but I need to find something more permanent and regular. I can supply you with good references from the three ladies I work for at present.'

'That all sounds fine to me. Would there be any problem over starting next week if we decide to take you on?' Rose studies Susan carefully, liking what she sees.

'No problem at all,' replies Susan. 'Are the hours definitely as stated in the advertisement?'

'Yes, unless someone is away. Would you be able to do extra hours if necessary?' Rose asks.

'Any overtime would be very handy. My girls are grown up now and can look after themselves when I'm not there, so I can fit in with you.' Susan smiles at her interviewer hoping she is showing just how eager she is to please.

'Right Mrs Prior. Well, I think that's all for now. Do you have anything you would like to ask me?'

Susan tries to think of the points she has jotted down. Most of them have been covered, except the embarrassing question about how much pay she will be receiving. She decides to ask. 'I hope you don't mind me asking, but could you just tell me what my pay will be?' Sue poses the question rather hesitantly, afraid she will spoil her chances of success.

'Oh, I am sorry, Mrs Prior, I should have told you that before. We pay our cleaners £3.50 an hour plus a bonus of £1.50 an hour for evening and weekend work. Does that sound all right to you?'

'Yes, that sounds fine, er, thank you.' Susan wonders whether to get up ready to go, but stays where she is until told.

'We'll be in touch with you tomorrow then, Mrs Prior. Thank you very much for coming.' Rose rises to her feet and shakes hands with Susan.

'Thank you for your time, Mrs Smith,' replies Susan. 'I look forward to hearing from you.' Susan remembers to smile as she goes out of the room.

Needless to say Susan gets the job!

THE APPRAISAL INTERVIEW

Most employees will attend an appraisal interview from time to time. These are usually held every six months or yearly. They are designed to assess the worker's progress, and usually take place between the employee and his or her immediate boss.

Your interviewer will highlight your achievements, and perhaps shortcomings, during the period under discussion. You will then have your turn to discuss your own views on progress, and to ask, should you wish to, if there are any chances of advancement within the company in the future.

If conducted properly, such interviews can help your career and make you feel you play an important part in the smooth running of the organisation.

Example of a successful appraisal interview

Jim Bruce, sales manager, is having his six month appraisal interview with Robert Power. Caravan sales are down and Jim is hoping he will not be in big trouble.

'Morning Jim, please come and sit down.' Robert greets Jim with a cheery smile which puts him at ease, at least for the moment.

'Now, Jim, time for your appraisal once more. How do you see your performance over the last six months?' Robert begins.

'Well, it has been a difficult period. As you know the recession is biting deeply in the country as a whole and people don't seem to have spare money to spend. . .'

'Yes, I know all that, but only *four* new vans sold in six months. That is disastrous, wouldn't you agree?' Robert interrupts in a rather irate voice, and Jim starts shifting about in his seat, feeling nervous once more.

'We have sold *twelve* agency sales secondhand vans though, and

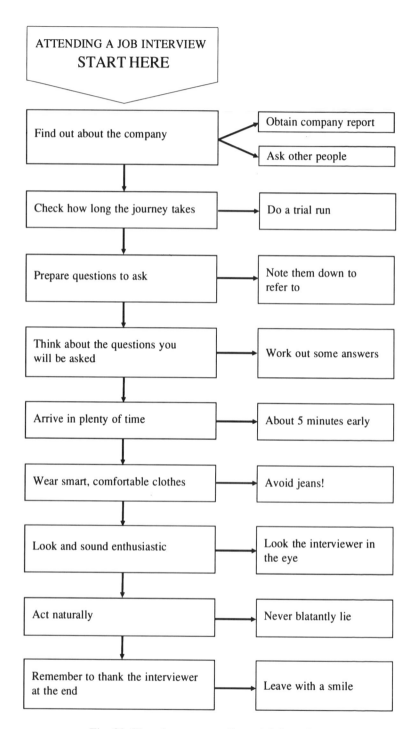

Fig. 30. Flowchart — attending a job interview.

that is twice as many as normal, which surely backs up my argument of there being no money around,' Jim counters, determined to hold his own.

'True, but we must find ways of encouraging more people to buy the new vans. What would you suggest?' asks Robert.

'Well, I thought we could arrange a caravan exhibition in July. I have spoken to Mike Reid at Mistleigh Caravans and he would be willing to let us have at least ten vans for one weekend. I also thought we could run a special finance deal at the same time. Perhaps we could even offer 0% finance over two years for any vans sold at the exhibition.' He looks at Robert seeking approval.

Robert nods. 'Good idea. Look Jim, I know you are a good man and you have done very well for us in the past. I'm sure you will turn sales around again, but this is no time to be complacent. You must be positive.'

'Look, Robert, my livelihood depends on selling vans. Without the commission on my sales we find it very hard to manage at home, so I can assure you I will do everything possible. Now I have your approval on doing something positive I feel a lot happier.' Jim feels confident he can make his future secure.

'I feel happier, too, Jim. I'm glad we've had this little chat. Let's see some action now so that in six months' time your next appraisal interview will be an occasion for celebration.'

The interview closes with both Jim and Robert feeling more confident about the future.

THE DISCIPLINARY INTERVIEW

The disciplinary interview is one of the hardest kind of interviews to either conduct or attend. It takes place when an employee has gone against company regulations in some way. It could be something relatively small, such as poor time-keeping, or something really major such as embezzlement of company funds.

Obviously it is far better never to have to attend such an interview, but if you do, make sure you are completely honest with the interviewer, answering all the questions put to you as well as you possibly can.

The interviewer on his or her part will be trying to get to the real reason for your misdemeanours. Organisations cannot be expected to tolerate unacceptable behaviour of any sort. On the other hand nor do they want to lose trained staff just because of a misunderstanding or a problem that can be easily sorted out. If you have recently been under a lot of stress due to family difficulties, or you feel you are being 'picked on' by another member of staff, tell the interviewer. It is your best chance of getting the matter sorted out once and for all.

If, at the end of the interview, both you and the interviewer feel confident that matters have been resolved, then the interview will have been worthwhile.

Example of a successful disciplinary interview

Ron Green, site foreman, has, on Robert Power's instructions, asked one of his maintenance staff, Paul White, to attend a disciplinary interview. Paul knows the reason why. It is because of poor time-keeping. He is very worried about losing his job.

'Come in Paul.' Ron ushers Paul into his little office and points to a chair. 'Now lad, Mr Power has asked me to talk to you. I think you know what it is about.'

There is a silence. Paul looks down at the floor not knowing how to word his defence. ·

'Yes, Ron. I do know what it's about. It's about the time I have been getting in each morning, isn't it? There are reasons though,' he adds, trying once more to think how best to put those reasons into words.

'I'm sure there are, lad. How about telling me about them then?' Ron settles himself back in his chair to listen.

'It's Jackie, the wife. You know we've not long had the baby. Well, Jackie hasn't been herself ever since. The baby cries a lot, especially at night, and I've often sat up with it for hours, so as Jackie can get her rest. Then in the mornings I always wake up late, absolutely exhausted, and Jackie cries when I say I'm going to work. I leave her every morning bawling her eyes out. I tell you Ron, it's really getting to me.'

Paul hates having to admit to Ron that he is not coping, but he needs to keep his job, so he has no alternative but to be honest. He looks at Ron to try and judge his reaction. He sees some sympathy for his plight so he carries on.

'I'm getting it sorted though, Ron. Can you give me another week?' Paul pleads. 'I took her to the doctor yesterday and he says this kind of thing is quite normal after having a baby, and that she needs some tablets and some extra help with the baby for a while. My mum has said she will help out and the health visitor is going to call in as often as possible too, so things will improve now.'

'Okay Paul. Let's give it another couple of weeks for you to sort yourself out. I think that's fair, don't you?' Ron looks relieved at the explanation.

'Thanks, Ron. I won't let you down,' says Paul as he leaves the room, grateful for the reprieve.

The interview ends with both men feeling the problem of lateness will now be resolved.

THE GRIEVANCE INTERVIEW

If you feel you are being unfairly treated by another member of staff, you should make a formal complaint to your employer. The interview that follows is known as a grievance interview.

The interviewer will be aiming to get at the truth. Tell him or her everything relevant to your complaint so that the matter can be fully investigated.

The next step is usually for the interviewer to see the person you have complained about, to find out their feelings on the matter. At that stage either the guilty party will be reprimanded, or the interviewer will bring both of you together to discuss what should be done.

There is absolutely no reason why you should ever feel unhappy at work because of the actions of others, so do not be afraid to ask for a grievance interview if you feel some positive action is called for.

Example of a successful grievance interview

Patsy Clark, telephonist, complaints to Susan Jones, office manager about the word processing operator, Sally Avery, treating her unkindly.

'So, Patsy, what's the problem? It must be pretty serious for you to request this interview,' begins Susan.

'Yes it is, Mrs Jones, or at least I think so,' replies Patsy, positively quivering with nerves. 'It's Sally. She's being really nasty to me all of a sudden.' Patsy's eyes fill up as she starts to cry.

'Don't cry, Patsy. Can you tell me in what way she is being nasty?' says Susan gently.

'Well, all of a sudden she just won't talk to me at all. However friendly I try and be, she just ignores me completely, and I've no idea what I am supposed to have done. When I ask her she still doesn't answer. I hate falling out with anyone,' finishes Patsy, starting to cry again.

'Sally can be a little quiet at times, Patsy, and I'm sure she doesn't mean anything by her actions, but I'll speak to her and let you know what she says.' Susan sounds reassuring and Patsy feels a little more confident.

'Thanks, Mrs Jones. I like my job, but I also like to get on with everyone more than anything else,' says Patsy as she gets up to leave. She hopes Mrs Jones will be able to help.

Mrs Jones speaks to Sally and then calls Patsy back into her office.

'Hello, Mrs Jones. You wanted to see me?' Patsy looks at her, almost frightened of what she will say.

'Yes, Patsy. Just to let you know that I have spoken to Sally and she is very sorry for upsetting you so much. Apparently, unknown to you, the boy you are going out with, I think his name is Dave, used to be her boyfriend. He gave her up and she is still very fond of him. When she heard he had taken up with you, she was so upset she just stopped talking to you. Plain jealousy, I'm afraid. Anyway, she sees now that she was wrong to take it out on you and she is sorry, so I don't think you will have any problems in the future.' Susan watches to see if Patsy seems relieved at the explanation.

'Poor Sally,' Patsy says immediately, full of remorse. 'I wonder why Dave never told me?' she continues angrily. 'That would have explained it all. Anyway, she's welcome to him and I shall tell her so. I was on the point of giving him up. I'm just glad it's all out in the open now. Thanks, Mrs Jones, for sorting it all out.'

'That's okay, Patsy. I've quite enjoyed playing the part of agony aunt, although I think in future romance and office life are best kept apart, don't you?' says Susan with a chuckle.

By the end of the second interview, the problem is solved and Patsy and Sally are able to work together in harmony once more.

ASSIGNMENT: BEING INTERVIEWED

Imagine you are Sally Avery, attending your first appraisal interview with Susan Jones. Bearing in mind the problems you have encountered with Patsy Clark, how would you see such an interview progressing? Write out a possible scenario.

PLANNING TO INTERVIEW SOMEONE ELSE

When you attend a job interview, probably your only thought will be to make a good impression so that you will be given the job on offer. You may give little thought to the effort that has gone into planning and structuring the interview in order for it to be successful.

When *you* are to be the interviewer, and have to plan an interview of any kind yourself, you will need to consider several points.

- The purpose of the interview. What do you wish to be achieved by the end of the interview? For instance with a job interview the end result is to appoint someone to the job on offer.

- The information required before the interview takes place. All the relevant information should be gathered together and read carefully as preparation for the interview.

- Questions to be asked at the interview. These questions will usually be compiled from the information collected and the notes made on that information.

- The time, date and place of the interview. The time and date will be arranged to suit all parties. The place of the interview will depend largely on the type of interview being held. Quite often an interview schedule will be prepared and circulated.

- The people who are going to attend for interview. It is most important that the interviewer spends some time researching the people he or she will be interviewing, so that as much as possible is known about them beforehand.

CONDUCTING AN INTERVIEW

When the interview takes place, perhaps the most important single point to bear in mind is that you, the interviewer, must try to adopt a friendly, relaxed manner in order to put your interviewee at ease. This will start the proceedings well, and set the scene for a successful interview.

- Work through the list of questions you have prepared beforehand in a logical order.

- Use 'open ended' questions as much as possible. These are questions which require more involved answers than a straightforward yes or no. They encourage the interviewee to express their views and feelings, for example 'Tell me why you left Green and Son?'

- Use 'closed' or direct questions where direct answers are required. Closed questions could be something like 'Do you live locally?' 'What qualifications did you obtain at college?' They enable you to work through a list of standard questions quickly, leaving more time for a general chat at the end.

- Make notes of the answers you are given.

- Show an interest in what the interviewee is saying at all times, by means of body language (nods and smiles) and by the use of encouraging words.

CLOSING AN INTERVIEW

When it becomes clear that all relevant points have been covered, you can bring the interview to a close.

- Summarise the main achievements of the interview for the benefit of both the interviewee and yourself.

- Explain any follow-up action to be taken.

- Thank the interviewee for attending.

Above all, make the interviewee feel that the interview has been a worthwhile experience, which, with proper advance planning, it will have been.

ASSIGNMENTS: INTERVIEWING OTHER PEOPLE

1. John Stein, one of the bar staff, has been acting very strangely over the past couple of months. He has been absent from work several times and is very quiet and withdrawn most of the time. As Bar/Entertainments Manager, what points would you wish to raise at a disciplinary interview?

2. Linda Grant is leaving Seaview. Assuming you are Robert Power, how would you conduct an interview for a replacement Personal Assistant? Write out the interview, particularly thinking about the special qualities needed for such a key position.

CHECKLIST

Being interviewed

- Have you thought about questions you might be asked?

- Have you thought of some questions of your own?

- Do you have all the relevant information to hand?

- Have you remembered to act naturally?

- Have you asked about any follow-up action?

- Have you thanked your interviewer on leaving?

Interviewing someone else

- Have you decided on the purpose of the interview?

- Have you obtained the necessary information?

- Have you arranged the day, time and place?

- Have you put the interviewee at ease?

- Have you used a variety of questions to maximum effect?

- Have you summarised the main points?

- What follow-up action have you decided on?

- Have you thanked the interviewee for attending?

POINTS FOR DISCUSSION

1. How would you answer the following questions at a job interview:

   (a) Tell me about yourself.

   (b) Why would you like this job?

(c)   Are you planning a family?

(d)   How do you get on with other people?

2.   Why is it important to tell the employer the truth at a disciplinary interview?

3.   When interviewing an applicant for a job, how would you begin the interview? How would you bring it to an end?

How to Know Your Rights at Work

Robert Spicer

A Practical Guide to Employment Law

'Clearly written in language readily understood by the layman . . . The text has been well laid out and sections are clearly signposted . . . The extensive use of case study materials is interesting and helpful . . . The book is not only relevant to Careers Officers and their clients, but also to other people working in the employment/ employment advisory field . . . The sort of book that can be easily dipped into for specific information, but which is interesting enough in its own right to be read from cover to cover.' *Careers Officer Journal.* 'Sets out in simple English everything an employee can expect in today's working environment.' *Kent Evening Post.* Robert Spicer MA (Cantab) is a practising barrister, legal editor and author who specialises in employment law.

£6.99, 141pp illus. 1 85703 009 5.

Please add postage and packing (UK £1 per copy, Europe £2 per copy, World £3 per copy airmail).

How To Books Ltd, Plymbridge House, Estover Road, Plymouth PL6 7PZ, United Kingdom. Tel: (01752) 695745. Fax: 695699. Telex: 45635.

Credit card orders may be phoned or faxed.

12
How to Master Grammar, Punctuation and Spelling

In this chapter we will discuss:

● is it worth bothering about grammar, punctuation and spelling?

● avoiding misunderstandings

● putting together sentences and paragraphs

● using parts of speech

● punctuating effectively

● words often misused

● common business spellings to know

WHY IS IT WORTH BOTHERING?

Several times during this book we have talked about the value of
creating a good impression. As far as written communication is concerned it is vital to have a good understanding of basic grammar,
punctuation and spelling. No-one is suggesting you should be a lite-
rary genius but care and attention should be paid to the construction
of all your written work. Well prepared, well displayed, error free
correspondence creates the impression of efficiency and a desire to
please. Both are very important in creating that good impression.

AVOIDING MISUNDERSTANDINGS

Written communication must be simply and clearly presented so that
the information given cannot, in any way, be misinterpreted.

Example

Jim Bruce, sales manager, sends the following handwritten note to Robert Power, general manager:

ROBERT:

I HAVE JUST HEARD FROM THE SMITH'S, PLOT 316. THEY ARE UNHAPPY ABOUT THE SITE FEES FOR NEXT YEAR. MR AND MRS JONES, PLOT 412 ARE TALKING ABOUT LEAVING TOO.

CAN YOU ADVISE?

Jim

Fig. 31. A confusing handwritten note.

What exactly does Jim want Robert to do?

* He says he wants him to 'advise', but what exactly does he mean by this?

* The Smiths are unhappy about the site fees, but Jim doesn't say what they (the Smiths) intend to do about it.

* He says Mr and Mrs Jones are thinking about leaving, but he doesn't say why. Do we assume it is because of the site fees?

* Why is the note so carelessly written? Couldn't Jim spare the necessary time and effort?

Example 2

Instead of the scrappy note, a proper memo, well constructed and clear in its meaning, would be much more suitable. An example is given below:

MEMORANDUM

From   Jim Bruce
To   Robert Power
Date   1 November 199-
Ref   JB/3619

There are two matters I would like to bring to your attention.

Firstly, the Smiths on Plot 316 have been to see me today. It would appear that they are unhappy about the increased site fees for next year. I think that unless we can justify the increase they will possibly leave.

Secondly, Mr and Mrs Jones on Plot 412 are also talking about leaving but for a different reason. They are worried about the new release of plots which they think will make the Park too large and impersonal.

Although I have done my best with both couples, I feel you should be aware of the situation. Perhaps a letter from you to both couples would help to persuade them to stay.

Fig. 32. A clearly expressed typed note.

Assignment

Referring to the rest of this Chapter when necessary for guidance on grammar and punctuation, compose a letter from Robert to both of the couples mentioned below. Explain that the increased site fees are due to higher water and electricity rates and also the new and improved facilities at the Park. The new plots will be the last to be created and there are only fifteen of them which should make no difference at all to the overall friendliness and personal running of the Park. Use today's date and the reference RP/CW. The names and addresses are as follows:

Mr and Mrs C Smith, 45 The Street, Roxley, Kent TN12 1YN
Mr and Mrs J Jones, 1 The Meadows, Wooton, Hants SO34 6NG

PUTTING TOGETHER SENTENCES AND PARAGRAPHS

All business text is made up of a series of sentences and paragraphs. It is important to understand the parts of sentences in order to be able to prepare them effectively.

What is a sentence?
According to *The Oxford Guide to the English Language*, a sentence is 'a set of words making a single complete statement'. To put it another way, a sentence must make sense and it must have a **subject** and a **predicate**.

● The subject is the person or thing being discussed in the sentence. It is normally a **noun** or a **pronoun** (see page 153 for explanation of nouns and pronouns).

● The predicate says something about the subject and it must contain a **verb** (see page 153 for explanation of verbs).

Example of a sentence

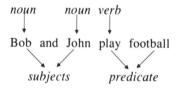

Sentences can be short or long, but never make them longer than necessary. Long sentences can be used in descriptive work. Short sentences are better for giving emphasis or a sense of urgency. Try to keep to just one item in each sentence, otherwise the meaning becomes clouded.

What is a paragraph?
A paragraph is one or more sentences grouped around a central theme or subject. When that theme or subject changes, a new paragraph should begin.

Every paragraph should have one sentence which describes the theme or subject for that whole paragraph.

Paragraphs can vary greatly in length, but generally speaking they should not be too long, or else the effect of the meaning is weakened.

USING PARTS OF SPEECH

There are different kinds of words known as the 'parts of speech'. It does not matter whether they are actually spoken or written down, they are still known by the same term. The main parts of speech are:

- nouns
- pronouns
- verbs
- adverbs
- adjectives
- prepositions
- conjunctions

Nouns
A noun is a name, either of a person or a thing. Only a proper noun needs to begin with a capital letter.

Examples
John Smith. (capital 'J' and 'S')
Saturday is my birthday. (capital 'S')

Other nouns such as man, dog, boy, begin with small letters.

Pronouns
A pronoun is a word used instead of a noun.

Example
John had a good idea. **He** gave the book to Jane. **She** put it in **her** bag.

Verbs
A verb is a 'doing' word. It shows action. It says what the subject of a sentence is doing. Every sentence should have a verb.

Examples
John **speaks** very clearly.
The child **ran** down the street.

Split infinitives

A split infinitive is when a word comes between 'to' and the rest of the verb. Generally speaking, this should not happen. For example:

She felt she ought **to** immediately **apologise** for the mistake. (*wrong way*)

She felt she ought **to apologise** immediately for the mistake. (*correct way*)

Adverbs

An adverb gives more information about a verb.

Examples
The child ran **quickly** down the street.
We **sometimes** drive to town.

Adjectives

An adjective is a 'describing' word. It gives more information about a noun. Do not over-use adjectives.

Examples
The apple was **crunchy** and **sweet**.
Susan was **thin** and **pale**.

Prepositions

A preposition shows how one thing or person relates to another. It is followed by a noun or a pronoun.

Examples
He reached **towards** her.
There was a gap **between** the door and the floor.

Conjunctions

A conjunction is a joining word.

Examples
Spot **and** Teddy.
He looked angry **yet** he said nothing.

Assignment

The following passage contains many grammatical errors. Ring round the errors and produce a corrected version. Remember to paragraph where necessary. Check against the perfect copy which follows after.

Uncorrected version

Seaview Holiday Caravan Park is set in rolling Sussex countryside, only a few miles from the sea. There is 200 acres to enjoy and explore and the holiday homes are situated on the most picturesque part of the Park, amongst trees, bushes, gentle screening. Everywhere you look there are a feeling of space and peace. The plots were all individual and carefully positioned so as to provide maximum privacy. Most of them has mains electricity and drainage and the few remaining plots without those services will shortly be connected. The Park itself offers a good range of facilities to suit all ages and tastes. There is a swimming pool, heated, and a adventure playground, complete with assault course. For the adults their was a bar and restaurant. Live entertainment was provided several times a week and their is a resident children's entertainer. Site fees include the use of the facilities, free, at all times when the site is open. Seaview Holiday Caravan Park offers the perfect choice for you and your family. We look forward to seeing you at our forthcoming caravan exhibition which was taking place next weekend, between 10.00 am and 1400 hrs on Saturday and Sunday.

Come and see us. You'll not be disappointed.

Corrected version

Seaview Holiday Caravan Park is set in rolling Sussex countryside only a few miles from the sea. There are 200 acres to enjoy and explore and the holiday homes are situated in the most picturesque part of the Park, amongst trees, bushes, and gentle screening. Everywhere you look there is a feeling of space and peace.

The plots are all individual and carefully positioned so as to provide maximum privacy. Most of them have mains electricity and drainage and the few remaining plots without these services will shortly be connected.

The Park itself offers a good range of facilities to suit all ages and tastes. There is a heated swimming pool, and an adventure playground, complete with assault course. For the adults there is a bar and restaurant. Live entertainment is provided several times a week and there is a resident children's entertainer. Site fees include the free use of the facilities, at all times when the site is open.

Seaview Holiday Caravan Park offers the perfect choice for you and your family. We look forward to seeing you at our forthcoming caravan exhibition which is taking place next weekend, between 10.00 and 2.00 pm on Saturday and Sunday.

Come and see us. You will not be disappointed.

PUNCTUATING EFFECTIVELY

Accurate punctuation is absolutely essential in business communication, otherwise the meaning of sentences can be completely changed. Take care not to over punctuate, particularly with commas. The following guidelines should help.

Capital letters
Capital letters are used:

- to begin sentences
- for proper names (*eg* John, Saturday)
- for titles (*eg* Mr)
- for acronyms (*eg* BBC, ITV)
- for days of the week, months *etc.*

Otherwise their use is often a matter of personal choice, but you should be consistent.

A full stop
A full stop is used:

- to mark the end of a sentence.
- It can also be used after initials, abbreviations or acronyms, although the modern trend is not to do so, preferring for example BBC to B.B.C. and Mr to Mr.

A comma
A comma is the shortest marked pause in a sentence and it is very widely used — sometimes too widely. Its main uses are as follows:

- To separate words or short phrases in a list. For example:
  The boy had blue, red, brown and green socks.

- To separate a word or words at the beginning of a sentence. For example:
  Regrettably, it was too late to do anything about it.

- To introduce speech. For example:
  She said, 'I hope you will all attend the meeting.'

- To separate something inserted into a sentence without changing the meaning of it. For example:
  It was not, however, an easy thing for him to talk about.

- To separate words which add extra explanation or meaning to the main theme. For example:
  The Mayor, who had been living in Africa, gave a very interesting speech on racial prejudice.

- To make a sentence generally easier to read and to avoid any confusion.

A semicolon

This is much more powerful than the comma. It has great value but is rarely used, mainly because it is not properly understood. It represents a longer pause than a comma but shorter than a full stop.

The main uses are as follows:

- To contrast two statements. For example:
  The lady liked the red dress; her husband preferred the black skirt.

- To separate items in a list. For example:
  The new swimming pool had luxury facilities: underfloor heating in the changing rooms; a jacuzzi and sauna; a fitness room; a marvellous water chute and a flume.

- To show statements closely linked in thought. For example:
  He hoped the figures would be better this year; life would be very difficult for him otherwise.

- To add emphasis. For example:
  Laura saw the man coming; he saw her face change; he ran towards her.

A colon

A colon has three main uses. They are:

- To introduce a list. For example:
  The films offered were as follows: My Dream by Mary Weldon, The Enchanted Haven by Susan Prior and Cannibal by Edward Plant.

- To introduce direct speech or a quotation. For example:
  Susan began her speech: 'My friends and fellow members will know how much this evening means to me.'

- To show two parts of the same sentence. The second part will normally explain the statement made in the first part. For example:
  June was a happy month for me: my hopes and ambitions came true at last.

Parenthesis or round brackets

The important point to remember when using brackets in a sentence is to make sure that it still makes sense if the words in brackets are removed. Generally speaking, the words in the brackets should add some extra explanation to the sentence. Do not use a capital letter for the first word in the bracket unless for a particular reason. Similarly, a full stop is not needed at the end of the bracketed words.

Example
Rachel Knight (the new committee member) will address the meeting next week.

Square brackets

These are rarely used. Their only real use is to show an addition to a direct quotation.

Example
Mr Black said in his report: 'I am so sorry about the downturn in trade this year. I hope that you [the employees] will understand our problems.'

The hyphen

The most common use of the hyphen is to join two words together so that they are looked upon as one. Nowadays, the hyphen in this form is fast disappearing and words that used to be divided are often shown as one word.

Examples
to-day is now today.
shop-keeper is now shopkeeper.

Times when hyphens are still used are as follows:

● Where the hyphen changes the meaning of the word. For example:
  recover — to regain possession, or return to health.
  re-cover — to re-cover something such as a chair.

● Instead of the word 'to'. For example:
  118-119 High Street.

● Dividing words at line ends. A hyphen is placed close up to the last letter of the line and the remainder of the word is carried on to the next line. Divide between syllables wherever possible. Unless there is already a hyphen in the word, *eg* re-cover, always leave at least three letters at the end of the line and carry over at least three letters to the next line. When using a word processing program, hyphenation can be set to operate automatically.

The dash
There are two kinds of dash, the single and the double dash. The main uses of the single dash are:

● To show a change of thought. For example:
  He stopped me on Monday — or perhaps it was Tuesday.

● To give an explanation. For example:
  His credit had been stopped — normal business practice in the circumstances.

The double dash can be used almost like brackets although it is more forceful. For example:
Two weeks ago — although it seemed longer — my mother left for Hong Kong.

His grasp of company business was good — or so he said — so I let him address the conference.

The exclamation mark
As its name suggests, this mark indicates an exclamation and it should be used very sparingly. Its general use is to inject humour into a sentence or paragraph.

The question mark

A question mark is shown at the end of a sentence which asks a question. It can also be used in business correspondence to show a query on a date or time *etc*.

Quotation marks

These marks are sometimes called inverted commas. Either single or double marks can be used according to preference, although it is more usual to use single nowadays except perhaps in direct speech. (This book uses single marks for direct speech.) If using a quote within a quote, use different marks for each.

Example
'I hope you will be able to see our new play ''The Last Train to Brighton'' on Sunday,' she said.

The apostrophe

The apostrophe is used in three main ways:

● to show the omission of one or more letters in a word. For example:
  I'm, he's, isn't.

● To show the possessive form. For example:
  Joanne's shoes, or the women's clothes.

● In names. For example:
  O'Grady.

If the apostrophe is being used to show the possessive use of a plural noun which already ends in 's', the apostrophe will be shown after the 's'. For example:
The lady's shoes. The ladies' shoes.

Note
It's and its are often confused. When the word is short for it is, it should be written with an apostrophe. For example:
It's a shame.

When it takes the possessive form meaning belonging to it, no apostrophe is needed. For example:
Its coat shone brightly.

Spaces to be left after main punctuation marks

There are many different ideas on the spaces to be left after full stops, commas, etc, when producing typewritten copy. The easiest method to remember is to leave two spaces after anything with a 'dot' at the bottom — in other words full stop, colon, question mark, exclamation mark — and one space after anything with a 'comma' at the bottom, in other words comma and semicolon.

Punctuation assignment

The following passage contains many punctuation errors. Ring round the errors and produce a corrected version. Paragraph where necessary. Check against the perfect copy which follows after.

Uncorrected version

The Minstral Bar at the Seaview holiday caravan park provides good beer, as well as good entertainment. Right through the season you can enjoy the very best selection of discos groups and cabarets. Where else in the Seaview area can you enjoy such pleasures. If you wish to eat there is a separate restaurant area booking is advisable where you can choose from a wide range of meals to suit the whole family. The delicious desserts include the following, Death by Chocolate. Lemon Cheesecake and seaview Ice Cream Surprise. On the first saturday of each month a special party evening is held You can join in the fun and games and possibly with a super prize. Well what are you waiting for. After all you are only young once.

Corrected version

The Minstral Bar at the Seaview Holiday Caravan Park provides good beer, as well as good entertainment. Right through the season you can enjoy the very best selection of discos, groups and cabarets. Where else in the Seaview area can you enjoy such pleasures?

If you wish to eat there is a separate restaurant area (booking is advisable) where you can choose from a wide range of meals to suit the whole family. The delicious desserts include the following: Death by Chocolate, Lemon Cheesecake and Seaview Ice Cream Surprise.

On the first Saturday of each month a special party evening is held. You can join in the fun and games and possibly win a super prize.

Well, what are you waiting for? After all, you are only young once!

WORDS OFTEN MISUSED

The following pairs of words are often confused. Take care to learn their different meaning and spelling.

Affect/Effect
Affect is a verb and mean 'to alter' or 'to change'. Effect can be a noun or a verb. As a noun it means 'result'. As a verb it means to 'carry out'.

Advice/Advise
Advice means 'opinion given' or 'piece of information'. Advise means 'give advice to' or 'recommend'.

Check/Cheque
Check means 'to test or examine for correctness'. Cheque is 'a written order to a bank to pay out money from an account'.

Council/Counsel
A council is 'an assembly'. To counsel means 'to give advice'.

Eligible/Illegible
Eligible means 'qualified to be chosen'. Illegible means 'unable to be read'.

Elicit/Illicit
Elicit means 'to draw out'. Illicit means 'unlawful' or 'not allowed'.

Personal/Personnel
Personal means 'one's own', or 'referring to a person'. Personnel means 'employees'.

Practice/Practise
Practice is a noun, as in 'the doctor's practice'. Practise is a verb and means 'to put into action'.

Principal/Principle
Principal means 'first in rank or importance', or 'capital sum of money'. Principle means 'general truth or doctrine'.

Stationary/Stationery
Stationary means 'not moving'. Stationery means 'writing materials'.

Their/There

Their means 'belonging to them'. There means 'in', 'at', or 'to that place', *etc*.

LIST OF COMMON BUSINESS SPELLINGS

There are a number of words that are frequently used in the business world, which seem to cause great problems when it comes to spelling them correctly. The following is a list of the most common of those words.

absence	efficiency	necessary
accessible	eighth	occasion
accommodate	elementary	occurred
acknowledge	embarrassed	omitted
acquaintance	enthusiasm	parliament
aggravate	equipped	permissible
agreeable	essential	privilege
all right	exaggerated	procedure
argument	expenses	professional
beginning	exercise	questionnaire
believed	extremely	receive
benefited	feasible	recommend
budgeted	February	reference
business	foreign	referred
category	forty	scarcely
colleagues	friend	schedule
coming	gauge	secretarial
committee	government	seize
compatible	grievance	separate
conscious	guarantee	sincerely
corroborate	honorary	successful
courteous	immediately	supersede
courtesy	independent	surprising
criticism	instalment	transferred
deceive	install	truly
decision	irrelevant	usually
definite	liaison	valuable
desperate	losing	view
disappointed	lying	Wednesday
disastrous	manoeuvre	
discrepancy	miniature	
dissatisfied	mortgage	

Assignment

Correct the incorrect words in the following passage. Produce a corrected version and check it against the perfect copy which follows
after.

Uncorrected version

Rose Smith will be holding a meeting for all cleaners on Saturday
20 March 199-. This meeting is neccesary due to a number of complaints from disatisfied customers last season. Most of the complaints ocurred during the busy months of July and August, but they
are still inexcuseable. A thorough cheque of the main complex will
take place daily and their will be no excuses excepted for poor
standards in the future.

Rose intends to advice the cleaners of there responsability to see
that the cleaning is carried out in a satisfactory manner.

Corrected version

Rose Smith will be holding a meeting for all cleaners on Saturday
20 March 199-. This meeting is necessary due to a number of complaints from dissatisfied customers last season. Most of the complaints occurred during the busy months of July and August, but
they are still inexcusable. A thorough check of the main complex
will take place daily and there will be no excuses accepted for poor
standards in the future.

Rose intends to advise the cleaners of their responsibility to see
that the cleaning is carried out in a satisfactory manner.

CHECKLIST

Think, whenever communicating on paper:

● Have you assembled the facts before starting?

● Have you written clearly and concisely to avoid misunderstandings?

● Have you made sure each sentence has a subject and a predicate?

● Have you kept to one subject for each paragraph?

- Have you used the parts of speech correctly?

- Have you punctuated effectively?

- Have you learnt the list of common business spellings?

- Have you checked unfamiliar words in a dictionary?

- Have you checked and re-checked your completed work for possible errors?

POINTS FOR DISCUSSION

1. Why is it so important for written communication to be accurately presented? Give five reasons.

2. What would your reaction be to a letter you received from a company containing many typing and spelling errors?

3. Do you think enough time is spent whilst at school learning grammar, punctuation and spelling?

Appendix 1

Decorations, Qualifications and Forms of Address

The dictionary defines 'decorate' as 'to honour a person by giving a medal or badge of honour'. Examples of decorations include KBE (Knight Commander of the British Empire), OBE (Officer of the Order of the British Empire) and VC (Victoria Cross). Decorations are shown before qualifications, and if more than one set of letters are to be shown, separate each set with a space. The modern trend is *not* to insert full stops after each letter. Some decorations carry a title: A person with a KBE would be called Sir.

Qualifications and honours show that the person has a degree, or other qualifications, and/or is a member of a professional body. Some qualifications mean that the person can use a title such as Doctor or Professor. Examples include: BA (Bachelor of Arts), BS (Bachelor of Surgery), MP (Member of Parliament).

ADDRESSING IMPORTANT PEOPLE

The Queen
It is usual to send a letter for The Queen to 'The Private Secretary to Her Majesty The Queen'. The letter should ask him/her to 'submit for Her Majesty's consideration (or approval)'.

If you do wish to communicate direct with The Queen, the following style should be used:

Beginning Madam
              With my humble duty

End   I have the honour to remain (or 'to be')
              Madam
              Your Majesty's most humble and obedient servant

Envelope   Her Majesty The Queen

166

Queen Elizabeth The Queen Mother
The same instructions apply as for The Queen, except that the phrase
The Queen Mother should be used.

Other members of the Royal Family
It is usual to write to the equerry, Private Secretary, or Lady in
Waiting of the particular member of the Royal Family.

If you do wish to communicate direct the following style should
be used:

Beginning Sir (Madam)

End   I have the honour to remain (or 'to be') Sir (Madam)
            Your Royal Highness's most humble and obedient ser-
            vant

Envelope His (Her) Royal Highness
            Followed on the next line by the name

The Prime Minister and other Members of Parliament
Beginning Dear (Name of Minister)

End   Yours sincerely

Envelope The Rt Hon (Name) MP

High Court Judge
Beginning Dear Judge *(excluding Surname)*

End   Yours sincerely

Envelope Sir Peter Jones

Circuit Judge
Beginning Dear Judge

End   Yours sincerely

Envelope His *or* Her Honour Judge Jones

The Pope
Beginning Your Holiness *or* Most Holy Father

End   *If Roman Catholic:*
I have the honour to be
Your Holiness's most devoted and obedient child
(*or* most humble child)

If not Roman Catholic:
I have the honour to be (*or* to remain)
Your Holiness's obedient servant

Envelope   His Holiness
The Pope

Archbishops of Canterbury and York
Beginning Dear Archbishop

End   Yours sincerely

Envelope   The Most Reverend and Right Hon the Lord Archbishop
of Canterbury/York

Priest
Beginning Dear Father Jones

End   Yours sincerely

Envelope   The Reverend Peter Jones

Vicar/Reverend
Beginning Dear Mr Jones *or* Dear Father Jones *or* Dear Vicar

End   Yours sincerely

Envelope   The Reverend Peter Jones

Duke
Beginning Dear Duke

End   Yours sincerely

Envelope   The Duke of Bath *or* His Grace the Duke of Bath

Wife of Duke
Beginning Dear Duchess

End   Yours sincerely

Envelope   The Duchess of Bath

Marquess, Earl, Viscount and Baron
Beginning Dear Lord Bath

End   Yours sincerely

Envelope The Marquess, Earl etc of Bath

Wives of Marquess, Earl, Viscount and Baron
Beginning Dear Madam *or* Dear Lady Bath

End   Yours sincerely

Envelope The Marchioness of Bath
            The Countess of Bath
            The Viscountess Bath
            The Lady Bath

Baronet
Beginning Dear Sir Peter

End   Yours sincerely

Envelope Sir Peter Smith Bt

Knight
Beginning Dear Sir Peter

End   Yours sincerely

Envelope Sir Peter Smith KBE

Dame
Beginning Dear Dame Susan

End   Yours sincerely

Envelope Dame Susan Moore DBE

National Vocational Qualifications

National Vocational Qualifications (NVQs) have been recently introduced by the National Council for Vocational Qualifications. They are available in many different subjects. Those intended to help office workers are Business Administration Levels I and II and Administration Level III.

Conventional examinations aim to test your formal skill and knowledge in one or more particular subject. NVQs are designed to prove that you can put your exam success to good use in the workplace. They deal with the practical aspects of your work.

NVQs are made up of different Units. Certificates can be awarded for just one or more Units, if you do not want to go on and take the full certificate.

Many of the topics listed below are included in the text of this book. If some of the words used here are unfamiliar to you, check in the glossary for their meaning.

BUSINESS ADMINISTRATION LEVEL 1

Unit 1: Filing

Element 1.1 File documents and open new files within an established filing system.

Element 1.2 Identify and retrieve documents from within an established filing system.

What you need to know

How to store information correctly.

How to classify, sort, handle and store documents.

How to follow the procedures of the organisation, including the handling of special and confidential files.

How to use different filing systems — alphabetical/numerical, vertical/lateral, card indexes.

How to operate a bring forward system.

How to use an absent card when removing files.
How to retrieve information.
How to plan and organise work within deadlines.
How to generally plan and organise the filing system.

Unit 2: Communicating Information

Element 2.1 Process incoming and outgoing business telephone calls.
Element 2.2 Receive and relay oral and written messages.
Element 2.3 Supply information for a specific purpose.
Element 2.4 Draft routine business communications.

What you need to know
How to use telephone directories.
How to speak clearly on the telephone.
How to listen carefully and take accurate messages.
How to operate installed equipment.
How to understand BT and other directories, systems and charge rates/costs.
How to answer the telephone in the correct way for the organisation you work for.
How to follow up telephone calls in the correct way for the organisation you work for.
How to follow up telephone conversation with confirmation letter, memo etc.
How to follow policy and procedures on security, safety and emergencies.
How to establish goodwill and a working relationship with colleagues and clients.
How to use an appropriate tone and style.
How to compose grammatically correct messages and notes.
How to locate people in your organisation and their responsibilities.
How to interpret oral and written messages.
How to liaise effectively with colleagues.
How to use dictionaries and other reference books.
How to plan and select presentation styles.
How to plan and organise work within deadlines.
How to spell and punctuate correctly.
How to plan and present business documents.
How to construct and present letters and memos.
How to identify the needs of the recipient.
How to use information sources, *eg* computer files, books etc.

Unit 3: Data Processing

Element 3.1 Produce alphanumerical information in typewritten form.

Element 3.2 Identify and mark errors on scripted material, for correction.

Element 3.3 Update records in a computerised database.

What you need to know
How to look after and use your machines.
How to operate a keyboard.
How to interpret oral and written instructions.
How to plan, layout, and correct your work.
How to save and print information.
How to spell and punctuate correctly.
How to use dictionaries and other reference books.
How to use a calculator effectively.
How to check your work.
How to make appropriate correction marks.
How to read and understand instruction manuals.
How to use appropriate correction marks.
How to follow the styles and formats of your organisation.
How to handle security and back up procedures.
How to diagnose faults in your system.
How to plan and organise work within deadlines.

Unit 4: Processing Petty Cash and Invoices

Element 4.1 Process petty cash transactions.
Element 4.2 Process incoming invoices for payment.

What you need to know
How to use a calculator.
How to complete simple forms and records.
How to operate a simple petty cash system.
How to communicate effectively.
How to maintain confidentiality.
How to understand the functions of purchasing/sales/accounts departments.

Unit 5: Stock Handling

Element 5.1 Issue office materials on request and monitor stock levels.

What you need to know
How to count quantities/estimate requirements.
How to use a calculator.
How to check the quality and condition of materials/equipment.
How to complete simple forms and records.
How to record, re-order and monitor levels of stocks.
How to locate and store the materials.
How to store and handle hazardous materials.
How to operate the legislation relating to receipt of goods.

Unit 6: Mail Handling
Element 6.1 Receive, sort and distribute incoming/internal mail.
Element 6.2 Prepare for despatch outgoing/internal mail.

What you need to know
How to use letter-opening equipment.
How to recognise unusual/suspicious items and how to report such incidents.
How to sort, attach, and distribute documents.
How to use a calculator.
How to complete simple forms/records.
How to plan and organise work within deadlines.
How to locate the people in your organisation and their responsibilities.
How to organise circulation lists.
How to deal with incoming mail.
How to extract information from reference books.
How to select suitable envelopes, packets and wrapping for despatch.
How to use scales, franking machine and weights and measures.
How to deal with outgoing mail.
How to send items by express delivery or courier.

Unit 7: Reprographics
Element 7.1 Produce copies from original documents using reprographic equipment.

What you need to know
How to read and understand instruction manuals.
How to recognise poor quality documents and equipment malfunctions.

How to operate and maintain commonly used reprographic equipment and materials.

How to collate, number and fasten papers together.

How to order materials.

How to compare costs of reprographic methods.

How to work within the copyright laws.

Unit 8: Liaising with Callers and Colleagues
Element 8.1 Receive and assist callers.

Element 8.2 Maintain business relationships with other members of staff.

What you need to know

How to listen to and interpret information.

How to interpret body language.

How to speak effectively.

How to maintain security and confidentiality.,

How to locate the people in your organisation and their responsibilities.

How to operate the telephone system.

How to deal with difficult visitors.

How to greet visitors.

How to liaise with senior colleagues.

How to interpret spoken and written requests.

How to plan and organise work within deadlines.

How to dress and behave correctly.

How to establish good relationships with colleagues and clients.

Unit 9: Health and Safety
Element 9.1 Operate safety in the workplace.

What you need to know

How to read and interpret instructions.

How to recognise and deal with potential hazards.

How to recognise the causes of hazards and accidents at work.

How to use safe working practices, including lifting and carrying of machinery/equipment/materials.

How to speak effectively.

How to complete simple forms/records.

How to operate a safety policy with clearly defined rules.

How to report and deal with an emergency.

How to locate and use fire fighting equipment.

How to locate and use alarms.

How to locate first aid equipment, and keep an accident register.

How to locate and identify a qualified first aider and safety representative.

How to appreciate the importance of safety legislation.

BUSINESS ADMINISTRATION LEVEL II

Unit 10: Creating and Maintaining Business Relationships

Element 10.1 Create and maintain professional relationships with other members of staff.

Element 10.2 Create and maintain professional relationships with customers and clients.

What you need to know

How to communicate and liaise with colleagues effectively.

How to plan and present information.

How to interpret spoken and written requests.

How to plan and organise work within deadlines.

How to dress and behave correctly.

How to locate the people in your organisation and their responsibilities.

How to use the internal telephone system.

How to interpret your and your employer's legal responsibilities under the Health and Safety at Work Act.

How to deal with difficult customers/clients.

How to interpret body language.

How to handle complaints.

How to greet customers and clients.

How to handle your legal obligations to the public, *ie* Public Liability, Trade Descriptions Act.

Unit 11: Providing Information to Customers/Clients

Element 11.1 Respond to customers/clients specific requests for information on products/services offered by the organisation.

Element 11.2 Inform customers/clients about available products and services.

What you need to know

How to communicate effectively.

How to deal with difficult customers and clients.

How to interpret body language.

How to interpret spoken and written information.
How to write a report/summary.
How to interview.
How to interpret the organisation's policy on disclosure of information.
How to greet customers and clients.
How to handle your legal obligations to the public, *ie* Public Liability and Trade Descriptions Act.
How to access paper based and computerised information sources.
How to locate information on products/services on offer.
How to understand the relevant aspects of the Financial Services Act.

Unit 12: Storing and Supplying Information
Element 12.1 Maintain an established filing system.
Element 12.2 Supply information for a specific purpose.

What you need to know
How to file correctly and accurately.
How to complete simple forms and records.
How to sort, handle and store documents.
How to index and cross-index.
How to deal with confidential files.
How to use different filing systems — alphabetical/numerical, vertical/lateral, card indexes.
How to operate equipment such as shredders.
How to operate a circulation list.
How to operate booking out and bring forward systems.
How to understand the relevant aspects of the Data Protection Act.
How to liaise effectively with colleagues.
How to use reference material.
How to interpret oral and written instructions.
How to present all written information, including graphs, charts, letters etc.
How to spell and punctuate effectively.
How to compose notes, letters, memoranda.
How to plan and organise work within deadlines.

Unit 13: Information Processing
Element 13.1 Process records in a database.
Element 13.2 Process information in a spreadsheet.

Element 13.3 Access and print hard copy reports, summaries and documents.

What you need to know
How to interpret written and spoken instructions.
How to use a keyboard.
How to understand business terminology.
How to plan and organise work within deadlines.
How to plan/match formats with software/hardware available.
How to proofread on screen and on paper.
How to operate and maintain all equipment safely.
How to operate security and back-up procedures.
How to name files and use formulae.
How to interpret the relevant aspects of the Data Protection Act.
How to operate a printer and diagnose printing problems.
How to retrieve information.

Unit 14: Telecommunications and Data Transmission
Element 14.1 Process incoming and outgoing telephone calls using a multiline or switchboard system.
Element 14.2 Transmit and transcribe recorded messages.
Element 14.3 Transmit and receive copies of documents electronically.

What you need to know
How to locate the people in your organisation and their responsibilities.
How to operate the telephone system.
How to use BT directories and codes, and internal directories.
How to clean and hygienically maintain equipment.
How to communicate with colleagues and callers effectively.
How to implement policy and procedures on security, safety and emergencies.
How to use the system at minimum cost.
How to operate and use an answerphone.
How to interpret written instructions.
How to project your voice.
How to operate a keyboard.
How to spell and use the English language effectively.
How to use accepted abbreviations and contractions.
How to plan and organise work within deadlines.

Unit 15: Reception
Element 15.1 Receive and direct visitors.
Element 15.2 Maintain reception area.

What you need to know
How to locate the people in your organisation and their responsibilities.
How to greet visitors and be aware of security, safety and emergencies.
How to take messages.
How to operate the telephone system.
How to use information sources effectively.
How to deal with difficult visitors.
How to explain the car parking arrangements available to visitors.
How to carry out the procedures of your organisation in maintaining the reception area and displaying notices.
How to acquire publicity material and stationery.
How to communicate and liaise with colleagues and visitors effectively.
How to compile and maintain organisation charts and internal directories.
How to achieve a well designed reception area.

Unit 16: Text Processing
Element 16.1 Produce a variety of business documents from handwritten/typewritten drafts.

What you need to know
How to use a keyboard.
How to look after your equipment.
How to interpret the different stationery sizes and qualities.
How to proofread on screen and on paper.
How to interpret different styles and formats.
How to interpret business terminology and English grammar.
How to use dictionaries, reference books and glossaries.
How to file and index.
How to interpret spoken and written instructions.
How to read and transcribe manuscripts and draft documents.
How to plan and organise your work within deadlines.

Unit 17: Audio Transcription
Element 17.1 Produce a variety of business documents from recorded speech.

What you need to know
As for Unit 16, plus
How to transcribe variable quality recorded material, containing alterations and additions/deletions.
How to use audio equipment, including safety and hygiene.
How to co-ordinate between audio equipment and a typewriter/word processor.
How to understand audio expressions used on tape.

Unit 18: Shorthand Transcription
Element 18.1 Produce a variety of business documents from dictated material.

What you need to know
As for Unit 16, plus
How to use one shorthand system.
How to develop shorthand vocabulary, short forms and phrases.
How to listen and memorise techniques.

Unit 19: Arranging Travel and Meetings
Element 19.1 Make travel arrangements and book accommodation.
Element 19.2 Arrange meetings involving three or more people.

What you need to know: travel
How to use information sources such as timetables, directories, maps etc.
How to deal with travel problems.
How to arrange travel documentation such as passports, travellers cheques etc.
How to use a calculator.
How to compose letters of confirmation.
How to arrange travel bookings.
How to operate the telephone, both nationally and internationally.

What you need to know: meetings
How to communicate effectively both orally and in writing.
How to identify requirements and calculate costs.
How to locate the people in your organisation and their responsibilities.
How to make effective use of information sources such as directories and reference books.
How to contact local suppliers, caterers etc.

How to organise the booking of meeting rooms.

How to understand the different types of meeting and meeting proto-
col.

Unit 20: Processing Payments

Element 20.1 Make and record petty cash payments.

Element 20.2 Receive and record payments and issue receipts.

Element 20.3 Prepare for routine banking transactions.

Element 20.4 Make payments to suppliers and others.

What you need to know

How to operate a petty cash system including recording procedures
and authorisations.

How to follow VAT guidelines.

How to undertake financial calculations (including use of calculator).

How to reconcile cash to records.

How to communicate effectively both orally and in writing.

How to achieve security in relation to cash handling and storage.

How to complete petty cash vouchers.

How to handle and store cash.

How to complete forms/records.

How to operate credit card imprinters.

How to plan and organise work within deadlines.

How to follow banking procedures, arrangements and documentation.

How to understand the use of foreign currencies/currency exchange.

How to complete cheques and counterfoils.

How to reconcile invoices, credit notes and statements.

How to interpret allowable discounts.

Unit 21: Processing Documents Relating to Goods and Services

Element 21.1 Reconcile incoming invoices for payment.

Element 21.2 Prepare and despatch quotations, invoices and statements.

Element 21.3 Process expenses claims for payment.

Element 21.4 Order office goods and services.

What you need to know

How to operate manual and computerised accounting systems.

How to understand the functions of purchasing, sales and accounting
departments.

How to use price lists, VAT guidelines, discounts and delivery charges effectively.

How to follow the procedures and documentation used in the organisation.

How to operate the filing systems.

How to make financial calculations and use a calculator correctly.

How to plan and organise work within deadlines.

How to communicate effectively both orally and in writing.

How to operate the organisation's code of practice for dealing with reimbursement of expenses.

How to record taxable and non-taxable expenses.

How to operate the organisation's procedures for order processing and emergency orders.

How to understand the sources of supply, catalogues, price lists etc, and the types of materials, services used.

How to complete the documentation of stockable and special items.

How to interpret the relationship between imperial and metric units.

How to operate the organisation's policy on quantity, quality, cost etc.

How to collect, classify and compare relevant information.

Unit 22: Processing Payroll
Element 22.1 Process documentation for wages and salaries.

Element 22.2 Process direct payment of wages and salaries.

Element 22.3 Arrange credit transfers.

What you need to know

How to make financial calculations, including the correct use of a calculator.

How to interpret information, *ie* clock cards, tax tables, NI tables.

How to complete forms and records.

How to operate manual and computerised payroll systems.

How to understand statutory and voluntary deductions.

How to understand banking/building society procedures.

How to follow the procedures and documentation used within the organisation.

How to follow the rules governing confidentiality.

How to follow the security procedure for cash handling and paying out the wages.

Unit 23: Maintaining Financial Records
Element 23.1 Maintain cash book, day book and ledger records.

What you need to know

How to follow the principles of double entry book-keeping.

How to follow the systems for describing and categorising purchases and sales under a variety of headings.

How to use manual and computerised accounting systems.

How to follow procedures and documentation used in the organisation.

How to use different types of ledger based systems.

How to follow VAT guidelines.

How to make financial calculations, including the correct use of a calculator.

How to communicate effectively, both orally and in writing.

How to compare and interpret numerical information from different sources.

How to plan and organise work within deadlines.

Glossary

Alphanumerical information	Information comprising letters and numbers
Acronym	Initial letters used as an abbreviation, such as VDU.
Answerphone	A device capable of recording telephone messages when no-one is available to take them personally.
Appraisal	Review of an employee's accomplishments.
Archive	File of often old information which may only need to be referred to occasionally.
Data	Information.
Database	Recorded data which can be retrieved and updated.
Deadline	Time limit.
Discriminate against	Treat unfairly.
Disk	Storage medium used by many computers. Can be 'floppy' or 'hard'.
Electronic mail	A method of communicating using computers linked by a telephone line.

Fax (Facsimile) machine	A machine capable of producing exact copies of documents and transmitting them via a telephone line.
Goodwill	Friendly feeling — established popularity and value of a business.
Hard copy	Printout (on paper).
Hardware	The mechanical, electronic and outer casing of a computer. If you can touch it, it's hardware.
Hazardous materials	Dangerous materials.
Health & Safety At Work Act	An Act passed to secure the health, safety and welfare of persons at work.
Interpret	Explain the meaning of something.
Ledger	An accounts book.
Legislation	Laws that have been made by parliament.
Mentor	Older or more experienced person responsible for guiding a less experienced person.
Program	The instructions written to make a computer obey certain commands.
Proofread	To check text carefully for mistakes.
Protocol	The correct way to do something according to rank or status.

Race Relations Act	This Act makes it illegal for an employer to treat an employee differently because of their race, colour or ethnic origin.
Rapport	Understanding relationship between people.
Recipient	Person who receives something.
Reconcile	To make two or more things agree.
Sex Discrimination Act	An Act of Parliament which makes it illegal for employers to discriminate against people on the grounds of their sex or because they are married.
Shredder	A machine used for cutting unwanted paper into unreadable shreds.
Software	The programs run on computer hardware.
Spreadsheet	An electronic worksheet containing data in various columns and rows which can perform automatic calculations.
Statistics	Collecting, sorting and interpreting information based on the numbers of things.
Telecommunications	Means of communication over long distances, eg telephone, fax, telex.
Terminology	The technical terms of a subject.
Transmit	To send or pass on.
VDU	Visual Display Unit — the screen of a computer.

Further Reading

The Cambridge Encyclopedia, edited by David Crystal (Cambridge University Press)

Communication, Nicki Stanton (Macmillan)

Communication for Business, Shirley Taylor (Pitman)

Debrett's Correct Form, edited by Patrick Montague-Smith (Headline Books)

How to Manage People at Work, John Humphries (How To Books)

How to Master Business English, Michael Bennie (How To Books)

How to Master Public Speaking, Ann Nicholls (How To Books)

How to Work in an Office, Sheila Payne (How To Books)

How to Write a Report, John Bowden (How To Books)

How to Write Business Letters, Ann Dobson (How To Books)

Practical Office Skills, Claire Taylor (McGraw-Hill)

Secretarial Duties, John Harrison (Pitman)

Success in Communication, Stuart Sillars (John Murray)

Index

How to Master Business English
Michael Bennie

Are you communicating effectively? Do your business documents achieve the results you want? Or are they too often ignored or misunderstood? Good communication is the key to success in any business.Whether you are trying to sell a product, answer a query or complaint, or persuade colleagues, the way you express yourself is often as important as what you say. With lots of examples, checklists and questionnaires to help you, this book will speed you on your way, whether as manager, executive, or business student. Michael Bennie is an English graduate with many years' practical experience of business communication both in government and industry. He is Director of Studies of the Department of Business Writing of Writers College, and author of *How to Do Your Own Advertising* in this series.

208pp illus. 1 85703 129 6. 2nd edition.

How to Master Public Speaking
Anne Nicholls

Speaking well in public is one of the most useful skills any of us can acquire. People who can often become leaders in their business, profession or community, and the envy of their friends and colleagues. Whether you are a nervous novice or a practised pro, this step-by-step handbook tells you everything you need to master this highly prized communication skill. Contents: Preface, being a skilled communicator, preparation, researching your audience, preparing a speech, finding a voice, body language and non-verbal communication, dealing with nerves, audiovisual aids, the physical environment, putting it all together on the day, audience feedback, dealing with the media, glossary, further reading, useful contacts, index. 'An excellent read — I recommend it wholeheartedly.' *Phoenix/Association of Graduate Careers Advisory Services*.

160pp illus. 1 85703 149 0. 3rd edition.

How to Pass That Interview
Judith Johnstone

Everyone knows how to shine at interview — or do they? When every candidate becomes the perfect clone of the one before, you have to have that extra 'something' to raise your chances above the rest. Using a systematic and practical approach, this How To book takes you step-by-step through the essential pre-interview groundwork, the interview encounter itself, and what you can learn from the experience afterwards. The book contains sample pre- and post-interview correspondence, and is complete with a guide to further reading, glossary of terms, and index. A Graduate of the Institute of Personnel & Development Judith Johnstone has been an instructor in Business Studies and adult literacy tutor, and has long experience of helping people at work.

128pp illus. 1 85703 118 0. 2nd edition.

How to Keep Business Accounts
Peter Taylor

The third fully revised edition of this easy-to-understand handbook for all business owners and managers. 'Will help you sort out the best way to carry out double entry book-keeping, as well as providing a clear step-by-step guide to accounting procedures.' *Mind Your Own Business*. 'Progresses through the steps to be taken to maintain an effective double entry book-keeping system with the minimum of bother.' *The Accounting Technician*. 'Compulsory reading.' *Manager, National Westminster Bank (Midlands)*. Peter Taylor is a Fellow of the Institute of Chartered Accountants, and of the Chartered Association of Certified Accountants. He has many years' practical experience of advising small businesses.

176pp illus. 1 85703 111 3. 3rd edition.

How to Master Book-Keeping
Peter Marshall

Book-keeping can seem a confusing subject for people coming to it for the first time. Now in a newly revised edition, this very clear book will be welcomed by everyone wanting a really user-friendly guide to recording business transactions step-by-step. Illustrated at every stage with specimen entries, the book will also be an ideal companion for students taking LCCI, RSA, BTEC, accountancy technician and similar courses at schools, colleges or training centres. Typical business transactions are used to illustrate all the essential theory, practice and skills required to be effective in a real business setting. Peter Marshall has been Tutor in Education at the University of Lancaster and Director of Studies at the Careers College, Cardiff.

176pp illus. 1 85703 065 6. 2nd edition.

How to Manage Computers at Work
Graham Jones

Most books on computers are highly technical, and often tied in to one particular application or product. This book really is different. Assuming no prior knowledge, it is a practical step-by-step guide which puts the business needs of the users first. It discusses why a computer may be needed, how to choose the right one and instal it properly; how to process letters and documents, manage accounts, and handle customer and other records and mailing lists. It also explains how to use computers for business presentations, and desktop publishing. If you are not sure how to start, then this is definitely the book for you . . . and you won't need an electronics degree to start! 'Bags of information in a lingo we can all understand. I strongly recommend the book.' *Progress/NEBS Management Association*. Graham Jones has long experience of handling personal computers for small business management and is Managing Director of a desktop publishing company.

160pp illus. 1 85703 078 8.

How to Do Your Own Advertising
Michael Bennie

This book is for anyone who needs — or wants — to advertise effectively, but does not want to pay agency rates. Michael Bennie is Director of Studies at the Copywriting School. 'An absolute must for everyone running their own small business . . . Essential reading . . . Here at last is a practical accessible handbook which will make sure your product or service gets the publicity it deserves.' *Great Ideas Newsletter (Business Innovations Research).* 'Explains how to put together a simple yet successful advertisement or brochure with the minimum of outside help . . . amply filled with examples and case studies.' *First Voice (National Federation of Self Employed and Small Businesses).*

176pp illus. 0 7463 0579 6.

How to Write a Press Release
Peter Bartram

Every day, newspapers and magazines are deluged with thousands of press releases. Which stories make an editor sit up and take notice? Why do some press releases never get used? The author knows from more than 20 years' first-hand experience in journalism what turns a release from scrap paper into hot news. This book takes you through every stage of the process from conceiving the story idea, researching the information and writing the release, to distributing it by the most effective means. If you have ever had a press release rejected — or want to win 'free' column inches for your organisation — *How to Write a Press Release* is the handbook for you. Peter Bartram BSc(Econ) is one of Britain's most published business writers and journalists, with more than 2,500 feature articles and seven books to his credit. He edits the magazine *Executive Strategy.*

160pp illus. 1 85703 069 9.

How to Write a Report
John Bowden

Communicating effectively on paper is an essential skill for today's business or professional person for example in managing an organisation, staffing, sales and marketing, production, computer operations, financial planning and reporting, feasibility studies and business innovation. Written by an experienced manager and staff trainer, this well-presented hand book provides a very clear step-by-step framework for every individual, whether dealing with professional colleagues, customers, clients, suppliers or junior or senior staff. Contents: Preparation and planning. Collecting and handling information. Writing the report: principles and techniques. Improving your thinking. Improving presentation. Achieving a good writing style. Making effective use of English. How to choose and use illustrations. Choosing paper, covers and binding. Appendices (examples, techniques, checklists), glossary, index.

160pp illus. 1 85703 124 5. 2nd edition.